Daisy Dress — For Zandra Rhodes

My favourite dress is the simplest. And that only happens after lots of complex designs — then a winner.

This vintage dress seems to have every thing I want to say. It is simple — chic + sexy + demands sensational legs — which is why I gave it to Bone Montague. Wore it and Orlena proposed. So Bone + Market Green have the most se... less. Mary (?)

The Ido dress from my Spring Summer 2002 collection was the first full length evening dress I ever designed.

Inspired by the philosophy of Madame Grès, its simply squares of black silk morrocaine, draped and constructed on the body, with a single seam.

When I made the dress I didn't view it specifically as an evening dress. It was more the fantasy of what fashion was all about when I was a child. For me as a man it defines the optimum balance between fabric and skin, which remains the core of how I design today.

I chose it for this exhibition as, even after all the other evening pieces I've done, I still get an immense thrill when I see it being worn.

FROM BETSEY JOHNSON...

Here we go with "Story" + Dress.

1 of a "Krazy-kinds tique" Betsey, Bunky, 9 — this is one of y.c.) I like range...it's m ess.... I was "skinny time. ar it

My favorite dress. Rarely is the little on its ex cial reward in its beauty, design or finish. has had a long quilted organdie dress I first made it in 1991. It seems to have as many stories as embroidered sequins. In the making, like the trange of dialogue has ou exc and three quilt making a different the dress emotion I've been told you can find their way tuck or used as shelter. It's been a wedding dress. The bride fell of such way down the aisle. She insisted I was being hugged and co and comforting of its bigness. So th a community powers. And this dress is "Favorite Dress" — Isabel Toledo

...the body, which eli up itself, offers itself to the d look with a wine. Fashion ...dress that make a dress, thou make a dress.

Sonia Rykiel

MY FAVOURITE dress

British Library Cataloguing-in-Publication Data
A CIP catalogue record for the book is available from the British Library.

ISBN 978 1 85149 592 4

Cover photograph: Golden Years, Celebrating 50 Years of Couture, British *Vogue*, October 2007
© Corinne Day / Maconochie Photography
Art direction and design by Robert de Niet, Samantha Erin Safer and Gity Monsef
Edited by Susannah Hecht

Typeset in Bauer Bodoni & Futura

Printed and bound in England by Butler Tanner and Dennis Ltd for
Antique Collectors' Club Ltd, Sandy Lane, Old Martlesham, Woodbridge, Suffolk, IP12 4SD

For every copy sold, the Antique Collectors' Club will donate 10% to Save the Children. All donations
to this charity help to make a lasting difference to children in the UK and around the world.

In every emergency, children are the most vulnerable.

WHEN disaster strikes, we need to be able to respond immediately. Children suffer in the critical
first days after an emergency and need our help straight away. Yet with the 2005 famine in Niger,
it took us two months to raise sufficient funds to intervene. We think that's outrageous.

YOU can enable us to help any child, at any time, by donating to the Children's Emergency Fund.
Having the funds in place before an emergency strikes means we don't lose precious time waiting
for the public or government support. We can get to work straight away.

We can't do this without your help. Working together, we will save more children's lives.

Save the Children®   Registered charity England and Wales (213890) Scotland (SC039570)

savethechildren.org.uk

MY FAVOURITE dress

Gity Monsef, Samantha Erin Safer and Robert de Niet

ACC Editions

Firstly, we would like to thank all the contributors to this book for providing us with their favourite dress and the very personal reasons behind it. We are indebted to our hardworking and amazing assistant Alice Cuffe for her dedication and enthusiasm. Deep gratitude to Suzy Menkes for writing such a beautiful foreword and her invaluable support for this project. We also extend thanks to Alexandra Shulman and her intimate essay expounding the love of dresses. We express thanks to Dennis Nothdruft for contributing an insightful essay and for his encouragement throughout this journey.

The contributors and the PRs have played an integral role in facilitating this book. Appreciation to Charlotte Przyiemski at Alberta Ferretti, Preia Narendra at Alexander McQueen, Peter Hermesdorf and Claire Joly at Anne Valerie Hash, Marisa Menzel at KCD PR for Anna Sui, Ali Lowry at The Communication Store for Amanda Wakeley, Antony Price, Barbara Hulanicki, Laura Gallacher at Bella Feud, Debbie Lovejoy at Ben de Lisi, Jutta Kraus at Bernhard Wilhelm, Agatha Szczepaniak at Betsey Johnson, Richard Hill at Betty Jackson, Tali Silver at Boudicca, Malcolm Carfrae, Jennifer Crawford, and Cari Engel at Clavin Klein, Jennifer Williams at Carolina Herrera, Hannah Widdecombe at Caroline Charles, Celine Danhier at Catherine Malandrino, Berangere Broman at Christian Lacroix, Suzanne Clements for Clements Ribeiro, Diane Pernet, Aude Casteja at Karla Otto for Diane von Furstenberg, Paola Locati and Marta Gallazzi at Dolce and Gabbana, Ellen Xiao Feng Guidone at Donna Karan, Daphnee Devichi at Dries van Noten, Chloe Constantinidi at Eley Kishimoto, Virginie Corré and Amy Strang at The Communication Store for Elie Saab, Daniela Ravaglia at Gianfranco Ferré, Kate Dooley at Giles, Amee Boyle at Giorgio Armani, Jennifer Dixon and Camilla Moshayedi for Glenda Bailey, Stephanie LaCava for Hamish Bowles, Jennifer DiPreta at Condé Nast Publications for Hamish Bowles, Suekay Kim at Hervé Léger BCBG Max Azria, Erika Stair and Meghan Horstmann at Isaac Mizrahi, Ruben Toledo at Isabel Toledo, Piera Beradi at Issey Miyake, Siobhan Mallen and Marc Morgan for Jane Bruton, Jenny Holland at Jasper Conran, Joe Casely-Hayford, Delli Avdali at John Galliano, Aileen Carville at John Rocha, Amelia Mullins at Julien Macdonald, Stéphanie Albinet and Hania Destelle at Lanvin, Victoria Hatcher at Louise Goldin, Gemma Corbett at Luella, Mark Flemming at Margaret Howell, Catherine Thomas and Marianna Protopapas at Maria Grachvogel, Carla Watt at Surgery PR for Markus Lupfer, Janey Bain for Mary Quant, Cat Staffell at Matthew Williamson, Chris Baker at Michiko Koshino, Alessia Minacapelli at Missoni, Siouxsie Webster at Moschino, Piera Berardi for Naoki Takizawa, Martha Platt and Holly Rakison at Nicole Farhi, Martha Botts and Valerie Veysseyre Constant at Pierre Balmain/Oscar de la Renta, Jet at Osman Yousefzada, Minh Lam at Paco Rabanne, Harriet Spense at BCPR for Paul & Joe, Laura Nicholson at Paul Smith, Sadie Mantovani at Ralph Lauren, Anne Ven der Bossche at Rick Owens, Ali Lowry at the Communication Store and Michelle Mahlke for Roland Mouret, Katerina Godi at Romeo Gigli, Pauline Klein at Sonia Rykiel, Hazel Cross at Karla Otto for Sophia Kokosalaki, Marina Cid at Stella McCartney, Cornelia de Uphaugh at Stephen Jones, Carole Varlot at Thierry Mugler, Alexandra Hill at Tracey Emin, Tristan Webber, Mita Guastella at Valentino, Marie Cuypers at Vera Wang, Cecilia Maresca at Vivienne Westwood, Susan Posen and Sarah Rosen at Zac Posen, Deborah Ababio for Zandra Rhodes.

We would like to extend our most sincere appreciation to Chris Moore for allowing the use of his catwalk images, which populate this book, and for supporting Save the Children in this endeavour. Appreciation to the photographers for allowing us to use their images to recreate the contributors' vision. Particular thanks go to Barry Lategan, Corinne Day, Corina Lecca, Dan Lecca, Dan Stevens, David Bailey, David Sims, James Mooney, Tiggy Maconochie and Helena Vidalic at Maconochie Photography, Peter Lindbergh, Niall McInerney, Marleen Daniels, Martin Brading, Mary McCartney, Rankin, Roger Prigent and Tim Bret Day. Many thanks to Ashley Macknica at Trunk Archive, Christine Cornetti at Michele Filomeno, Melissa Regan at Art and Commerce, Sam Beckett at Mary McCartney, Zoe Roberts at Chris Moore, the Metropolitan Museum of Art, and Condé Nast.

Special thanks are extended to Carmen Ho for her assistance at the beginning of this project and also to Anette Wilms. We acknowledge Hilary Davies and Seth Dagger.

We want to thank from the bottom of our hearts James Smith of the Antique Collectors' Club for giving us this opportunity, championing the book, and for his complete support throughout the whole of this project, as well as the many cups of coffee. We thank the Antique Collectors' Club, especially Diana Steel, our editor Susannah Hecht, Alison Hart, Anna Morton, Jo Lord and the rest of the team for bringing this book to fruition. Special thanks to Madeleine Ginsburg and Audrey Barrett. A big thank you to Mark Eastment for spearheading this book many years ago and for his continued guidance. Special thanks to Deborah Lampitt for her kind input and Louise Simmonds for her council. Appreciation to colleagues at V&A Publishing for their advice and guidance.

Working with Save the Children has really touched us and we thank Lynn Whittaker and Stefanie Rees for all their passion and hard work in securing this great partnership as well as Jasmine Whitbread, CEO of Save the Children.

Lastly, we are very thankful to our families: Nicholas de Niet, the Monsef family, Gary Webb, Robin Safer and Rita Shapero for their love and encouragement.

OUR *FAVOURITE* *thanks*

This book would not have been possible without the support of fashion icon Zandra Rhodes CBE and the Grand Opening Exhibition of the Fashion and Textile Museum 'My Favourite Dress', curated by Gity Monsef with assistant curators Tim Hunter and Louise Stocks-Young and curatorial support from Samantha Erin Safer. The ground-breaking exhibition which forms the basis of this book was achieved through the support of Zandra Rhodes and Salah Hassanein. Founders of the museum – we thank you.

Gity Monsef, Samantha Erin Safer and Robert de Niet

foreword:
MY FAVOURITE
dress

Suzy Menkes

Fashion Editor, *International Herald Tribune*

"Emotion reflected in tranquillity" was the definition of poetry from that great romantic writer William Wordsworth.

Anyone who has bought a dress with wild passion and seen that emotion continue to flow gently each time it is worn, will understand the warmth with which so many fashion enthusiasts have contributed to this exceptional book.

For designers, a creation can seem like a child: it becomes a living object that grows and changes over the years – as with the dress that Isabel Toledo first made in 1991 – and that continues to seem relevant today. Stefano Gabbana and Domenico Dolce think back to the first time they brought together the sacred and the profane – their image of a woman in a curving guepiere corset, her sensuality purified by the innocence of a rosary. For John Galliano, the arch romantic, a dress is always designed to give women a dream, as roses embrace the shoulder and tumble over slithering silk.

Behind every favourite dress there is one defining word: emotion. It might come from a bridal gown that caught in its taffeta folds the magic of an unforgettable day. Or it could be a more banal memory of the luck an outfit brought to an interview for a new job. Or it might be just a particular wardrobe piece that always brings a sense of comfort and confidence. For most people who are not connected to the fashion business, the strongest link is between the dress and a particular person or event.

But for me, the most potent memory goes back so far that I know the date – 1972 – only because it is written beside David Hockney's signature on a drawing of Celia Birtwell, the wife of the late Ossie Clark.

The picture hangs on my bedroom wall. And although it is in shades of grey lead pencil, I can see in my mind's eye the colours of the clustering bouquets of meadow flowers on the wispy white chiffon ground. I can feel the full sleeve billowing over my arm, but caught in at the wrist so that I could show off the gold watch that was a present for my 21st birthday. A part of my life is in that dress, which was surprisingly versatile, in that after I wore it to my engagement party, it then got me through three pregnancies, as I loosened the half-sash that tied in a bow at the back.

I remember so clearly that fashion moment, when Ossie's long, sinuous silhouettes ushered in a new fashion era after the angular, geometric sixties. I am sure that if I contacted Celia Birtwell – who is still the imaginative fabric designer she was then – she would tell me about the inspiration of the flowers. And she would recall how still she stood as she was sketched by David Hockney – the artist being part of the 'Mr and Mrs Clark' circle.

The drawing went on the programme cover for Ossie's fashion show at the Royal Court Theatre, Chelsea, where the Beatles and their girlfriends sat front row. I took it reverentially home and framed it back then.

Now, every time Naomi Campbell sees me, she asks me when I will sell her the 'Ossie dress'. Sell it? I couldn't bear to give it away – even if it is just slumbering inside tissue paper in a long box in the upper reaches of my wardrobe.

It isn't, after all, any tired, old dress. It is as much an object of desire now as when I bought it in Ossie's little shop off London's King's Road. It has a beating heart inside it. Or perhaps the heart is mine.

MY FAVOURITE introduction

Gity Monsef and Samantha Erin Safer

Gity: We all have a Favourite Dress, currently mine is a blue sleeveless cotton shirtwaist dress with gold buttons that cinches my waist and lies perfectly over my hips. I had worn this dress many times before it became my favourite: to a christening, to my birthday drinks, to an opening… And then boom! In an instant it was my favourite; because it was the blue dress that I happened to be wearing when my boyfriend got down on bended knee and asked me to marry him (and I accepted). The moment, the place, the atmosphere, the situation – it has all been etched in my memory forever. I love that dress because of that moment and how it makes me feel every time I wear it – special and loved; it takes me back to one of the greatest moments of my adult life. I can foresee myself keeping this dress forever.

Samantha: I am one of those girls who is a dress girl. I would rather wear a dress than any other garment – it makes me feel sexy, powerful, beautiful and always chic. Rather like Bernhard Wilhelm (who has chosen six favourite dresses as his contribution), I have many favourite dresses: my party dress (Gold by Giles from his first New Look collection) with its bright polka-dot print moulded into a strapless corseted confection with black patent belt and short puffball skirt; the black crêpe babydoll-style dress with fine pin tucks at the bodice that my mother bought for me when I was 13 to wear to bar and bat mitzvahs, which I still cherish and wear today. Then there is my favourite day dress for winter: a hunter green wool knit dress with a stand-up collar and ruching on the left side from Diane von Furstenberg (her clothes fit my curves perfectly); and for summer, a colourful patchwork dress that brings me such joy. I could go on...

* * *

This book is a celebration of the dress, the most important item in any woman's wardrobe. That piece of clothing that is so much linked to feminine sensibilities, maturation, and an item donned for almost all occasions.

The seed for this book was planted years ago when we had the opportunity to delve into the archive of the iconic British textile designer Zandra Rhodes. The archive housed over 3,000 beautiful creations from the softest printed chiffon, to shimmering gold pleated silks, and early experiments with feathers and quilting. We wondered to ourselves: if Zandra had to choose her favourite dress, out of all the collections and dresses she had designed since launching her label in 1969, which one would it be? And what would others in the global fashion industry choose as their favourite dress? This simple question has led to the opening exhibition of the Fashion and Textile Museum in London, and now this wonderful and insightful book.

As the dresses, stories and pages unravel, they display the power of a moment or moments in one's life, design career or memory. The book has thus become a commentary on the emotional attachment or bond that various personalities – designers, artists, stylists and fashion editors – have with the one thing that is treasured in their memory or wardrobe: their favourite dress.

When collating this book, we had one criterion: the designers had to choose a favourite dress they had designed themselves. The other contributors from the industry were asked to choose their favourite dress from their own wardrobes or another's collection. The selection is fascinating, the dresses chosen by these individuals highlight the intimacy that the designers and the wearers feel about each garment and the choices embody their design aesthetic. Each dress that was submitted would lead us into deep discussion, evoke surprise, or would take us back to our own fashion memories. For example, before he passed away, Gianfranco Ferré himself chose the red crêpe dress with gold foil embroideries that was immortalised by Carla Bruni on the catwalk for his autumn/winter 1992/1993 collection – we remember that dress, it was elegant, powerful and incredibly sexy.

Paco Rabanne submitted a modern day version of his iconic dress fashioned of plastic and metallic grommets, which debuted in 1967. This updated piece of fashion history, now made of plastic sequins and mother-of-pearl shell, reminded us of the futuristic design experiments from the late 1960s and the power of creativity and its timelessness. The making of sensational images, when the designer, the dress, the model, and the photographer come together, is what drove Donna Karan to her favourite dress, which she designed in 1996. The beautiful cut and fabric of her green dévoré dress was a perfect fit on Demi Moore, who was shot in it by Peter Lindbergh for the Donna Karan ad campaign – a series of images that we think captures a true fashion moment of the nineties. Glenda Bailey, editor of *Harper's Bazaar*, writes of wearing her favourite dress on the momentous occasion of her 50th birthday and how she felt, succinctly recalling these intimate feelings. The wearability, the feeling, the dress, the designer and identifying with the designer in a very personal way are all shown through her choice.

The contributors have set the theme for the book and, in a way, they have become the authors – the pages are filled with their words, their inspiration, their images, personally selected to represent their favourite dress. What emerge are snapshots into each contributor's feelings towards the design process, making, inspiration, wearing and above all design sensibility.

This book affords us an opportunity to explore how a dress can be a creative statement, a symbol of celebration, power and individuality. A favourite dress is about choice, memory and a moment.

THE WOW factor

Alexandra Shulman
Editor of British *Vogue*

There's something special about wearing a summer dress, making you feel removed from the pressures of life.

I used to own the perfect summer dress. It was navy blue silk with small white flowers, little capped sleeves, a fitted bodice and it swirled narrowly rather than frumpily around my mid calves. I was in my 20s and the general fashion of the day was skewed towards short skirts and sharp-shouldered jackets, but this dress by Edina Ronay made me feel wonderful whenever I wore it.

Therein lies the mysterious power of the summer dress. If you, like me, are a "dress" person you will know what it is that a dress, quite unlike trousers, skirts, shorts, blouses and jackets brings to the way you feel. It offers the promise of a life that is deliciously removed from the pressures of every day, the repetitiveness of routine, the need to be somewhere, do something, that makes up so much of our time, and transports you instead to something far more enjoyable and gracious. It allows you to dream, to slow down – to be girlish, even.

Of course, everybody's perfect dress differs and, looking back, I find it somewhat strange that it was such a conventional, covered-up dress that gave me so much pleasure when I was young, but I think that the feeling of femininity, the pure prettiness of it and the sexiness of being bare under the silk probably made up a large part.

Even now, nearly 25 years later, my wardrobe holds not exactly copies, but substitutes for that dress. Yet none has achieved the same level of perfection. As a child, longing to get out of scritchy and confining winter clothes, I seemed always to be told, "N'er shed a clout till May is out", or was it June? Every year I can never quite remember, as I dither about whether it is too early to pack up the winter clobber and unwrap summer, which is how it feels when one replaces the winter woollies in the drawer with T-shirts and sarongs.

As soon as the clocks change I crave those dresses, bundled up in polythene bags at the top of the cupboard, that will emerge crumpled and smelling faintly of the suntan lotion that has permeated my holiday wardrobe stuffed up there with them.

Summer dresses are completely different from winter dresses, which, although they should offer the same one-stop ease when you are thinking about what to put on in the morning, somehow seem to bring with them more problems. What tights to wear? Should it be boots or shoes? Will you need a jacket and a coat? You just slither into the ideal summer dress and that's it.

At the optimum summer-dress occasion a fortnight ago, my friend's annual croquet match, most of the women were in dresses. Anna Sui, Diane von Furstenberg, Cath Kidston – all of us wafting, because surely that is one of the things a dress allows you to do, in prints that ranged from ditsy florals to brash brushstrokes, hair piled up in dishevelled nests, arms uncovered.

The arms question, of course, exercised everybody. It's a toss-up whether women are more concerned about baring their arms or their legs but it is undoubtedly true that it is hard to find summer dresses that help with either of these concerns. I seem to remember that you used to be able to easily find versions of land-girl style shirtwaisters, or short-sleeved, vintage-influenced tea dresses falling to beneath the knee, but dresses now have become most disobliging. They are short – too short for many women – often slashed down the front necessitating a vest or T-shirt underneath, and almost all sleeveless.

For those who really want cover, there are dresses that can help. The shirtwaister, although a rare breed, does exist; some of the most lovely are by S-Sung – heavy cotton, fitted tightly up top and often in oriental inspired prints. Then there are tunic-style dresses with kimono sleeves (these work best if you can keep a bit of leg showing), and there are Grecian-inspired smocks. Scanning my wardrobe, I find my new purchase – a fine Indian silk print dress with small capped sleeves – seems to be doing sterling service in the heat (it's by a brand I had never heard of, called Matta), as is a longsleeved cotton dress by Thakoon with a ravishing ink blue tie-dye. Bought last year, it is still a favourite. There are a couple of Marni finds – a very fine artist-style smock

dress and a short-sleeved summer frock that I keep mainly because I know one day, with its pattern of naively drawn roses, it will make a beautiful lampshade.

Most dress-buying nowadays is accompanied for many women by "top" buying as well, to compensate for the lack of dresses with sleeves. Boleros, shrunken cardigans, Chanel-style jackets, short coats – all of these are on offer as accompaniments. But the very fact of needing or wanting them destroys some of the unique appeal of summer dresses. You should not have to wear them with anything else.

Sleeves, on the other hand, need not compromise the summeriness of a dress. Sleeves are many women's security blankets, soothing and protective. There is something cosseting about a soft, billowing sleeve after a day in the sun or on the beach. There is an elegance about the bracelet-length sleeve, which delightfully throws the emphasis on the thinnest part of the arm – the wrist – while covering the fleshy upper arms so many women hate. One of my own favourite dresses is a decade-old black one from Ghost that has elbow-length sleeves and which, I like to think, has a touch of the glamorous Italian widow about it Claudia Cardinale would be a nice reference point. Otherwise, the short cape is helpful for day dresses that otherwise might make you feel too exposed.

My arms are less my personal area of anxiety than my legs, not entirely helped by

Hardy Amies once telling me as he tucked into his pre-lunch martini that the ugliest part of a woman's anatomy was the knee. I think he was wrong in this observation but not every woman looks her best wearing hems above the knee (particularly minus the camouflage of tights). The current fashion length tends to cut off at the lower thigh, exactly the point in most women where the legs widen. Why would you want to draw attention to it? Despite this, you will find it hard this summer to find a dress to reach the knee.

Although I am amazed to find myself writing this, leggings seem suddenly to be a bearable solution to wear under dresses if you find the seasonal loss of the opaque tight unsurvivable. The 80s revival has made them fashionable again and although they can never, ever be regarded as flattering or sexy, they do help on days you simply can't face bare legs. At least they allow a flash of ankle, possibly some calf, and hopefully they will be worn with open-toed sandals. (I am a great believer in the power of the heel to help out with legs.) Over the years I have kept a large collection of dresses. Even those I can no longer wear remain with me, loved for their memories, their colour and in hope that maybe next month or next year I might be able to wear them again. If not, they still please the eye, like paintings.

What works and what doesn't continually changes. I have a number of dresses by Legacy, an American brand stocked by the Cross in Notting Hill, west London. For several years they were perfect. With slightly capped sleeves, a bias cut, a low neck and in a variety of feminine but not sickly silk prints, they ticked a huge number of boxes. But they are slightly high-waisted, almost empire line, and as time passes this silhouette becomes, shall we say, more challenging.

A dress you once imagined as delightfully bohemian suddenly looks like something your least favourite teacher would wear on the hottest day of term. Because summer highlights not only concern about bare arms and legs but seems to draw unwelcome attention to the depth of your torso. The distance between the front of your stomach and your back unfortunately becomes a whole new difficult territory delineated by the thin fabrics of summer, and high-waisted dresses do little to help this.

But all of these caveats are just quibbles. Whatever the shape, colour, fabric, or length or your summer dress, the main point is that it is so much more than the sum of it and your parts. When you find the right one it is like a new lover – the world just seems a better place.

THE FAVOURITE *dress*

Samantha Erin Safer and Dennis Nothdruft

The idea of a favourite dress, for some, is the simplest of questions – the dress and its image spring immediately to mind. For others, deep thought, soul searching and digging around one's closet or studio are needed to gain an answer. The transforming properties of this feminine garment are embedded in the cut, silhouette, and colour that fashion designers so carefully create and construct. Style the dress up, style it down, a favourite dress can be a woman's secret weapon. But what does a favourite dress mean and how does a favourite dress come into being?

My: *adj.* The possessive form of I. Favourite: *adj.* something regarded with special favor or liking. Dress: *n.* Clothing; apparel or a style of clothing: *folk dancers in peasant dress* as well as a one-piece, outer garment for women or girls. Can also be an outer covering or appearance; guise: *n.* an ancient ritual in modern dress. *i*

My Favourite Dress. The meanings of these words, when explored, all emphasize the personal, yet are embedded with the historical in their etymology. For instance the word *'my'* developed around 1200 as *mi,* a reduced form of mine used before words beginning in consonants except *h-* (*my father, but mine enemy*), and before all nouns beginning in the fourteenth century. *'Favourite'* was first recorded in 1583, from old French *favorit* a variant of *favori,* the past participle of *favorir* "to favour" or give favour to the king, a race, a fight or a woman; favour was later applied to material possessions, places or experiences. It is when we pause and investigate the vari-

ous instances of the word *'dress'* that one gleans insight into how it has come to express both clothing the body and a form of design and communication.

The history of the word *'dress'* has an interesting past and not one that typically comes to mind. A dress is such a common article of modern attire that it is difficult to imagine that the word *'dress'* has not always referred to the garment. The earliest noun sense of *'dress'*, recorded in a work written before 1450, was "speech, talk". This *'dress'* comes from the verb *dress*, which goes back through old French drecier, "to arrange", and the assumed vulgar Latin *directiare to Latin directus, a form of the verb dirigere, "to direct". In accordance with its etymology, the verb *dress* has meant and still means, "to place", "to arrange", and "to put in order". The sense "to clothe" is related to the notion of putting in order, specifically concerning clothing. This verb sense then gave rise to the noun sense "personal attire" as well as to the specific garment sense. The earliest noun sense, "speech", comes from a verb sense having to do with addressing or directing words to other people.

Therefore, dress at one time represented communication, and a *dress,* an outer garment worn by women and girls, a statement made tangible, giving form to thought and feeling; not always an overt statement but a coded message that can be read, or misread, by those around the woman so adorned. It is through this medium that we can all find something to say, speak of some secret place that we may never verbalize, and can use to signal to others our hopes, desires, and even fears. The act of choosing then becomes the creation of the outer self, a designed object.

If thinking of clothing oneself as an act of arrangement and arranging objects together (which is a choice all of us make, consciously or unconsciously every morning), we design our visual statement of purpose for the day. This act of arranging can be seen as our defense and justification to a society that we may or may not feel comfortable in. The dress as an object has always been equated with women; the dress being the basis of perceived values of womanhood as well as the foundation of the woman's wardrobe since clothing existed. However, the women's wardrobe has since vastly expanded, more so than traditional men's clothing with its prescribed set of limitations; women on the other hand now have the battlefield of not just clothing the self but navigating the depths of fashion. Hence, the choice of a dress, traditionally a feminine object, places a woman in the context of traditional roles. It is the modern woman who takes that object, and through her arrangement of it, either claims as her own the inherent feminine power, or rejects those contexts and instills the dress as an object with her own values, codes, and identity.

Thus, the historical and the conceptual become the personal. Our selection of a favourite dress, though underpinned by deep historical associations, becomes cherished as something we love and have a personal attachment to. A favourite dress, 'my favourite dress', has strong connotations that are special and specific to and for each wearer and possessor of a favourite dress. To put on the favourite dress is to know that one will feel instantly confident, beautiful, lifted – acknowledging the power that a favourite

dress has. The dress slides over the body, the zips or hooks are done up and instantly the wearer is transformed into their own ideal of beauty. Beyond this transformation is how the dress defines the wearer, communicating various ideas and images to the world.

Social philosopher Giles Lipovetsky writes 'haute couture unleashed an original process within the fashion order: it psychologized fashion by creating designs that gave concrete form to emotions, personality, and character traits."[ii] Though a favourite dress is not necessarily haute couture, Lipovetsky points to how clothing oneself and more specifically picking a favourite dress speaks about the wearer's being; what their emotions, moods and character traits are. This dates back to the convention of society portrait painting when women and men were not necessarily painted in their favourite suit or dress but in their 'best'. Seeing these images repetitively have formed the basis of our idea of putting one's best foot forward, special occasion dressing or Sunday best, not necessarily implying that the favourite is the finest or best that one owns.

Some favourite dresses are only donned once or twice a year for a special occasion; pulled out from the back of the closet and brought back into the world. This type of favourite dress has deep memories attached to it, such as one's graduation, a ball, a wedding, or an opening. The owner of the favourite dress knows exactly how many times it has been worn, when and where, who was there and the atmosphere – all these details becoming woven into the dress, expanding the meaning of it being the favourite, embedding it with a history. There is also the impulsive purchase of a dress, which slowly becomes the favourite. A purchase made to satisfy the need for a bit of retail therapy with no premeditation.

The owner wears the dress, is complimented, feels confident and attractive thus impregnating the dress with positive associations that are recalled every time the dress is worn. Another facet is the familiar becoming the favourite; comfortable, chic, sexy, cool, powerful, and personal. The wearing becomes as much of the overall creation as the initial design or idea, thus embedding the garment with one's own memories and restarting the cycle. The cyclical fashion of favourite dresses changes as we change, though maintains a constant thread. Roland Barthes writes 'the theatre of fashion is always thematic: an idea (or, more precisely, a word) varied through a series of examples or analogies."[iii] This creates a dialogue with us and the past favourite informs the newest love; fashion design is then seen as an externalisation of the interior discourse.

Beyond exploring the personal, the lens can be turned on the creator, bringing a new element of discovery to our understanding of 'my favourite dress'. To ask designers to choose their favourite dress, from their own work, represents, in effect, a summation of each creator's design, culture, and world view. The reasons behind the choice of each dress speak of the myriad of inspirations and instigations that make up a garment. Christopher Breward writes about a 'symbiotic relationship that existed between idea, object, and image in the system of couture,' and for many designers their favourite dress is a reflection of just this – a moment in time, a particular 'snapshot' that symbolizes an instant where design and desire merge with the woman wearing it, and her place in the universe.[iv] This moment can also be a pure fashion moment, on a catwalk or in a photograph, which for the designers crystallizes their own place and their vision of themselves.

Such choices are intensely personal to the designer, but may be as profound as an 'ultimate' in their design careers, or for no deeper thought than "it worked". As our personal favourites can change for private reasons, the designer's favourite can change as his or her personal working style evolves or vocabulary expands with experience. The very nature of the act of design in the studio or workroom creates its own momentum, necessitating change in the designer's personal best. Nonetheless, the designing spirit is essentially restless and one needs to question whether a designer can even have a favourite dress? Can the designer pin down one garment out of the many created or is there one from each collection representative of the moment of inspiration? If using a muse, preconceived notions of internal and physical beauty as well as inherent style play a significant role in the selection of a favourite, thus the muse is married to this ideal and only exists within this system.

When it comes down to it, the choice of "My Favourite Dress" lies deep within us. We can tease out these ideas and stories, gaining an insight that we did not possess. The exploration of the designers' choices creates a new dialogue between the objects, the process, and a constant conversation we have within ourselves.

[i] Dictionary.com Unabridged

[ii] Giles Lipovetsky, *The Empire of Fashion: Dressing Modern Democracy*, Translated by Catherine Porter, (Princeton & Oxford: Princeton University Press, 1994), p. 79.

[iii] Roland Barthes, *Systeme de la mode*, Paris: Editions du Seuil, 1967, *The Fashion System*, Translated by Matthew Ward and Richard Howard, (Berkeley, Los Angeles & London: University of California Press, 1983), p. 301.

[iv] Christopher Breward, 'Intoxicated on Images: The Visual Culture of Couture', in *The Golden Age of Couture*, Claire Wilcox, ed (London: V&A Publishing, 2007), p. 185.

alber elbaz for lanvin, alberta ferretti, alexander mcQueen, amanda wakeley, angela missoni, anna sui, anne valerie hash, antonio berardi, antony price, barbara hulanicki, bella freud, ben de lisi, bernhard willhelm, betsey johnson, betty jackson, boudicca, calvin klein, carolina herrera, caroline charles, catherine malandrino, christian lacroix, clements ribeiro, daisy de villeneuve, david sassoon, diane pernet, diane von furstenberg, dolce & gabbana, donna karan, dries van noten, eley kishimoto, elie saab, francisco costa for calvin klein, gianfranco ferré, giles deacon, giorgio armani, glenda bailey, hamish bowles, hamish morrow, isaac mizrahi, isabel toledo, issey miyake, jane bruton, jasper conran, joe casely-hayford, john galliano, john rocha, julie verhoeven, julien macdonald, louise goldin, luella bartley, margaret howell, maria grachvogel, markus lupfer, mary quant, matthew williamson, max & lubov azria for hervé léger, michiko koshino, naoki takizawa, nicole farhi, oriole cullen, oscar de la renta, osman yousefzada, paco rabanne, paul smith, pearce fionda, ralph lauren, rick owens, roland mouret, rossella jardini for moschino, romeo gigli, sonia rykiel, sophia kokosalaki, sophie albou for paul & joe, stella mcCartney, stephen jones, thierry mugler, tracey emin, tristan webber, valentino, vera wang, vivienne westwood, zac posen, zandra rhodes.

THEIR FAVOURITE *dresses*

alber elbaz
for lanvin

My Favourite Dress: Alber Elbaz for Lanvin, Autumn/Winter 2002, Silk tulle with wool jersey

A dress is not designed for a star, for the moon or for the clouds. I design for women and whether they are rich and famous, blonde or brunette, it should not be my observation when the piece has been taken out of the kitchen of fashion. I love dresses because they are effortless. You zip it in and you zip it out. You do not have to stylize it; you do not have to think period! You have to feel and look like a woman. In this particular dress, I exercised a story of contradiction. A ballerina dress in grey and not in pink! A mix of fragile tulle with a masculine jersey. Contradiction is what modern life is all about.

alberta ferretti

My Favourite Dress: Alberta Ferretti, Spring/Summer 2002, Silk chiffon with ruche details

When I create my collections, I always have the image of a moving silhouette and the chiffon tissue perfectly depicts the lightness and the fluidity I search for. It interprets in the best way the Ferretti style. This is a dress from the Spring/Summer collection, that comes from an inspiration stimulated by Edward Weston's images, so immaculate that they seem like poetry applied to photography and above all the beautiful pictures he took of skies and clouds touched me. This energy of harmony and dream combined with an always sensual and elegant femininity, generated my imagination and stimulated the creation of a dress that really belongs to me.

alexander mcQueen

My Favourite Dress: Alexander McQueen,
Autumn/Winter 2002/03,
Lace chiffon and satin corset

With this favourite dress, there is a sexiness in the structure of the corseting mixed with the softness of the dragonfly lace and ruched chiffon.

amanda wakeley

My Favourite Dress: Amanda Wakeley,
Spring/Summer 2009, Satin twill

*Here the values of a timeless Amanda
Wakeley satin twill dress are modernised by
the suggested sexiness of the cinched waist
combined with fluid skirt. Amanda Wakeley
loves "the original, modern femininity of this
dress. The papaya colour makes a great
statement. I danced 'til dawn at a New Year's
Eve beach party in Mexico wearing this
dress over my bikini."*

angela missoni

My Favourite Dress: Angela Missoni,
Missoni, Autumn/Winter 2000,
Viscose with Swarovski crystal

*The transformation of the Missoni essence
is in this favourite dress. My "space-dyed"
pattern and long "scarf" morphs into a
glamorous evening dress with glittering
Swarovski crystals. The dress softly gathers
at the waist from a light band, with a deep
V-neck obtained by two long scarves
wrapping around the neck.*

anna
sui

My Favourite Dress: Anna Sui,
Spring/Summer 2001, Silk

*This trompe l'oeil dress from my Spring
Collection is like a cartoon of my ultimate
dream dress. With its white collar and cuffs,
the girl wearing it becomes an Anna Sui
cartoon character complete with artwork
drawn by Chooch.*

anne valerie hash

My Favourite Dress: Anne Valerie Hash,
2001, Suiting fabric

*This is my favourite dress as it is the first dress
I designed at the beginning of my fashion
adventure, back when I launched my house
in 2001. This dress made me famous –
It is a pair of men's trousers transformed into
a woman's dress. The dress was a huge
success when it was created and it is still
one of our best sellers and my favourite.*

antonio berardi

My Favourite Dress: Antonio Berardi, Spring/Summer 2002, Cotton lace with cut-glass buttons

The dress was really a last minute thing, made of cotton lace (exclusively woven in the north of England for ecclesiastical use) and literally thrown together during the fittings for the Spring/Summer show.

Metres of lace edging were sewn together to form the skirt and sleeves and a punched cotton bolero-cum-waistcoat with cut-glass buttons thrown over the top to finish it off.

This white sugary confection proved so popular that after the show three more were made to satisfy the demands of the press. Not bad going, considering it was born out of nothing, and my favourite for this reason.

antony price

My Favourite Dress: Antony Price, Silk

This is my favourite dress of the moment because it embodies flattering shape and form with architectural drama without compromising its sexuality – one of the most difficult combinations to achieve. As usual, my inspiration came from leaf forms found in natural Caribbean plants, but the resulting design began to bear a resemblance to the Sydney Opera house, which was also probably inspired by nature. I came to design this dress for a fashion show in Barbados. It was to be worn by a tall, very long-necked Barbadian girl. Consequently, the pale pistachio green and the light summery weight of the silk coupled with the tall elegant shape and the dramatic wrap made it look exquisite as it glided between huge, backlit exotic plants. As a designer, I judge purely by its structure and resulting impression rather than the social status of the wearer. Indeed the social status of the wearer should be elevated by the dress not the dress elevated by the wearer. The garment does not dramatically alter its form because someone famous wears it – its job is to make someone quite ordinary look quite famous.

barbara hulanicki

My Favourite Dress: Biba, 1968, Velvet

My inspiration for this favourite dress was Princess Margaret as she always had on wonderful coat dresses.

bella freud

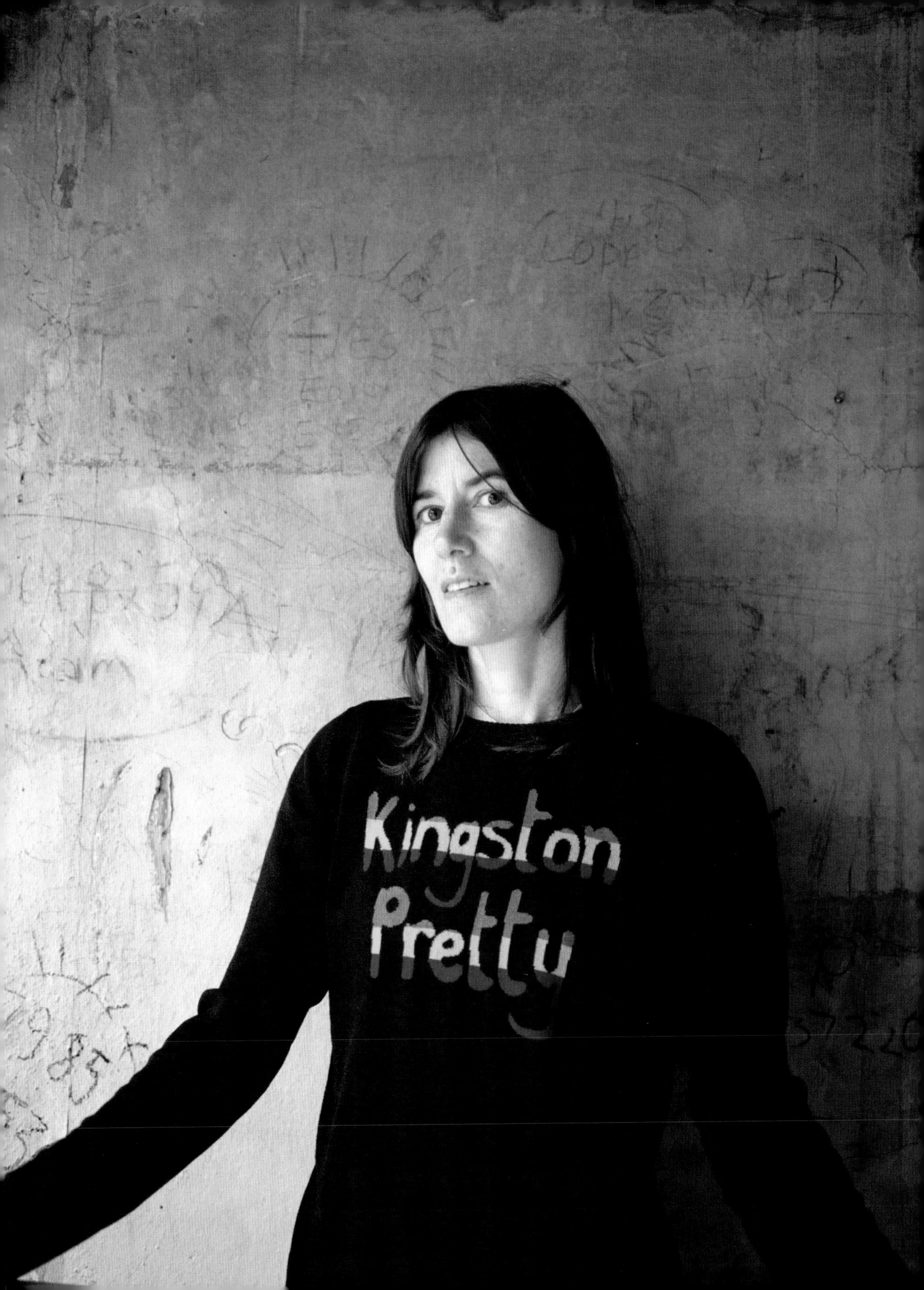
Kingston
Pretty

My Favourite Dress: Bella Freud,
1992, *Belle de Jour Dress*, Knitted

*At the time of designing this dress in 1992
I was looking at the film* Belle de Jour *and
Catherine Deneuve, admiring the subtle way
she projected being demure and overt.
I wanted the dress to convey some of that.
The dress is very simple but it makes you
look again. The model is Susie Bick who also
captivated these qualities, she was wonderful
to work with, in fact we are designing a
collection together for Spring/Summer 2010.*

ben
de lisi

My Favourite Dress: Ben de Lisi,
Autumn/Winter 2002, Crêpe with foil
printed panels made from satin-backed
pebbled crêpe

*Trying to decide which of the many, many
dresses I have designed during my career
is my favourite was a task unto itself.
Rails of styles to choose from – how do you
select just one? Well, I wanted a dress that
spoke volumes about what I think "Ben de
Lisi" means. Fluid, long, lean, sexy, chic
architecturally cut, with impact – a dress that
caressed the body. A dress to make you
stand different, walk different, make you shine.
This dress embodies all of these qualities.
It is strong, feminine, relaxed and slinky.
For me it is timeless, at home, on the
beach or at a ball. The gold foil was
inspired by drawings of Bentwood
Danish rocking chairs, taking components
of the curves, twists and circular movements.
Choosing the fabric was easy, crêpe was
the base, and metallic gold was classically
beautiful and showed off the foil print best.
The style had to be sexy, strapless, figure
skimming, with masses of long floor-dragging
skirt for the perfect entrance or exit. Since
I created this dress, it has been one of my
rules to measure other dresses by. It remains
effortless, exciting, and most of all unique.*

bernhard willhelm

My Favourite Dress: Bernhard Willhelm

A Dress for Dead
Autumn/Winter 2007/08

A Dress for a Box
Spring/Summer 2007

A Dress for Jutta
Autumn/Winter 2008/09

A Dress for Bernhard
Spring/Summer 2009

A Dress for Bjork
2007

A Dress for Two
Spring/Summer 2007

betsey johnson

My Favourite Dress: Betsey Johnson,
1972, Grand Canyon Dress,
Wool jacquard knit

This dress was part of a series of "Save the Planet" knits I designed in 1972 for Alley Cat. Other visuals knitted into sweaters were birds, butterflies, shells, vegetables, baby animals and storks. These sweaters won me the major fashion industry award of its time… The "Coty Award". The knits were made in knitting factories in Philadelphia, which are long gone now. It has always been a favourite of mine.

'ALLEY CAT' 1972
GRAND CANYON
(FRONT)

betty
jackson

My Favourite Dress: Betty Jackson,
Spring/Summer 2002, Silk

*When we started thinking about this Summer
Collection, we had been talking in the studio about Chinese textiles and details. Then
we saw the film* In the Mood for Love, *and
found it completely inspirational, as it seemed
to crystallize all our thoughts. It was beautiful,
sexy; self contained and vulnerable; special
and surprising all at the same time, and
it became one of our reference points
throughout the season. The dress sums the
whole thing up and is a favourite from that
collection.*

boudicca

Our Favourite Dress: Boudicca,
Autumn/Winter 2003, *Darko Dress*,
French lace

Susan Sontag tells us – 'Fashion is fashion photography'. Justin Smith took a photograph of this fine lace skin disguise and immortalised it in a cell of ink, a last cigarette, a sexual, sensual moment of loneliness in front of a lens. That is when the dress came alive, became a favourite. When it belonged to the world as something more than just another dress or catwalk moment. Of course, this image was never published as part of an editorial, it was taken because Justin wanted to and that makes all the difference. A shot at the end of the day, an image for himself, given to us.

calvin klein

My Favourite Dress: Calvin Klein,
Autumn/Winter 1999, Paper radzmire

The idea behind this black paper radzmire slip dress is that it is folded and layered to sculpt the body. It gives the evening dress modern clarity. It is elegant, self-assured, and sexy.

carolina herrera

My Favourite Dress: Carolina Herrera, 1992, Evening suit designed for Jacqueline Kennedy Onassis, Satin jacket with embroidery by LeSage with velvet skirt

The evening suit belonged to Jackie Onassis and it is one of my favourite ensembles that I have designed. I asked Jackie Onassis for a dress for my archives and she sent me back two; this evening suit being one of them. I will eventually donate them to a museum in her memory, but for now I hold on to them to remind me of our great friendship.

On 23 April 2001, I wore a modified version of this evening suit to The Metropolitan Museum of Art's Costume Institute Gala "Jacqueline Kennedy: The White House Years" in honour of her.

caroline charles

My Favourite Dress: Caroline Charles,
1995, Silk chiffon with beading

*My favourite dress is this black and gold
dress, which suggests Cleopatra or Maria
Callas. It is for a diva on a grand occasion,
definitely for a performance.*

*The cut is slender and simple. It is perfectly
arranged to show a woman's body to
its best advantage. The fabric is silk and
the bead and sequin work is Byzantine
yet modern.*

Caroline CHARLES

Caroline CHARLES

catherine malandrino

My Favourite Dress: Catherine Malandrino, Autumn/Winter 2001, *Flag Dress*, Silk and chiffon

When I was preparing for my Autumn Collection in 2001, I was inspired to create a dress that celebrated freedom through the image of the American flag. I designed the dress six months before September 11th and due to the tragedy, the dress became an icon that portrayed the essence and patriotic mood of New York and of America as a unified nation.

For me, the dress combined my French style-ideology with the cut of the dress and my American style-ideology because of my love of tie-dye and the symbol of the American flag. This dress played a special role in fashion after September 11th. Women such as Chrystèle Saint Louis Augustin, Halle Berry and Kathy Hilton all gave the dress their own special individual flare. Chrystèle wore the dress open to the waist with her nude chest bared in the front, Halle sheared off the sleeves and Kathy accessorized with diamonds.

christian
lacroix

My Favourite Dress: Christian Lacroix,
Haute Couture Collection, Autumn/Winter
2000/01, Embroidered satin, chiffon
and organza

*What I have always preferred for the past 15
years is when a dress matches or surpasses
the sketch. When the initial anecdote, story or
theme transforms itself into a moving sculpture
revealing the body by changing its silhouette
with majesty (which is the aim of couture)
and mixing the abstract and the baroque,
the architecture and the decor, the minimal
and the maximal to create a favourite dress.*

clements
ribeiro

Our Favourite Dress: Clements Ribeiro, Autumn/Winter 1997, *Carnation Dress*, Chiffon with embroidery

The "Carnation Dress" is a purely personal choice of ours. Over the years we have done many challenging or extravagant pieces which would probably make more striking display. This dress however, is cherished by us as a perfect example of a certain brand of 'clumsy' and effortless femininity that has become an essential part of the Clements Ribeiro style. A simple shift dress made of two layers of satin finished silk georgette, embroidered with red shredded chiffon and green viscose ribbon, a delicate row of red glass beads topstitching the neckline and armholes, it looks almost home-made. Worn with hand-painted 'tattoo' tights and spiky Mary Jane stilettos it expresses many modern contradictions of romance and femininity, as well as an attitude towards dressing up and decoration, which sharply reflect our design vision.

This dress was a key piece from our "Punk Trousseau" Collection (Autumn/Winter 1997/1998), worn by Audrey Marnay on the catwalk. It was a seminal collection for us in which many elements first experimented with then turned out to become Clements Ribeiro staples. The heady mix of unrelated inspiration starting points (Punk London, Victorian Trousseau, '20s flapper dresses, '40s tea dresses, bohemian styling, 'home-made' embroidery...) reached a certain level of accumulation that became intrinsic to our work process from then on. The show also featured the famous 'Union Jack' sweater, modelled by Naomi Campbell, an emblematic image used many times over to represent the cultural moment of that time, the so-called "Cool Britannia". The "Carnation Dress" though, in its fragile beauty, remains our personal favourite, then as well as now.

daisy
de villeneuve

My Favourite Dress: *Vintage Dress*, Bought in London at Rellik in 2000, Silk

My favourite dress is a vintage turquoise dress with a Chinese inspired print that I bought at Rellik in the Golborne Road in 2000. It was my first trip to the shop and I was picking out something to borrow for a British Vogue feature entitled, "Cool Girl Gangs" in London, which was photographed by the US photographer Pamela Hanson. At the time, I was living on Portobello Road in the heart of Notting Hill with my sister and friends, we wore clothes from the market there (only shopping on Fridays as that was the best time to go) or charity shops; our clothes were second hand and cheap. We could not afford designer items and did not want to wear high street clothing and look like everyone else; we wanted to be individual. My sister and I soon became known for our style and our more unusual dress sense.

The dress did not end up in the final shoot that day for Vogue, but I loved it so much that I decided after the photo shoot to go back to Rellik and buy the dress. I remember being concerned that I was buying an expensive dress, I was used to spending £3 on dresses not £60, therefore I was hesitant, but now I'm ever so pleased. I've had the dress for several years now and it always comes out for a special occasion, a birthday, wedding, cocktail party, charity event or New Year's Eve. When I first wore the dress I had dyed brown hair to cover the two-tone colour in my hair that was underneath, I used to wear purple fishnet tights and high heels. Now my hair is long and blond and the fishnets have been thrown aside but the high heels are a must.

david
sassoon

My Favourite Dress: Bellville Sassoon -
Lorcan Mullany, Spring/Summer 1989,
Satin and silk tulle

*This rose chine satin silk dress is from the
Spring/Summer 1989 Collection and is
my favourite dress. The romantic mood of
the collection was perfectly captured in a
photograph of Blaine Trump dancing with
Mikhail Baryshnikov at the Gala opening
of the American Ballet theatre season at the
Metropolitan Opera House.*

diane pernet

founder of
a shaded view on fashion

My Favourite Dress: Haider Ackermann,
Autumn/Winter 2009, Mixed wool

*I love the way the fabric drapes sensually over the body.
The back view is as outstanding as the front. What I like
especially about Haider Ackermann's work, and this favourite
dress in particular, is that it is sensual but never touches on
vulgarity. The dress is cut on the bias and I imagine draped
directly onto the body in the same way as a signature
Madame Grès. Let's say that Haider Ackermann is a modern
day Madame Grès. Timeless designs that bring out the inner
goddess of a woman.*

diane
von
furstenberg

My Favourite Dress: Diane von Furstenberg,
Spring/Summer 2002, Silk jersey, vintage
link print from the 1970s

*The wrap dress in the link print, a dress
created many years ago, a print created
many years ago, is back in style for a
whole new generation. The wrap dress is
a favourite dress, a dress that does not
need buttons, a dress that embraces the
shape of the body and sculpts it, allowing
it to move. The fabric, silk jersey, is soft
enough to feel like a second skin and dry
enough to hold perfectly.*

*The print is geometric and bold, but the
movement of it is fluid and flattering.
It is a very unassuming dress, it does not look
like much on a hanger, but on the body it
becomes magic – it takes the personality of
the woman it dresses, it envelopes the body
in a very becoming way. It is a dress that
makes women confident, and confidence
is the first step to beauty, many wonderful
things happen when you wear a wrap dress.
So, feel like a woman and wear it with joy...*

Feel like a
woman,
Wear a dress!
Diane Van Furstenberg

dolce & gabbana

Our Favourite Dress: Dolce & Gabbana, Spring/Summer 1990, Stretch cotton and satin with silk crochet shawl

In our imagination, the guêpière dress is the quintessence of the Dolce & Gabbana style. Since the beginning of our career, in our early collections, we tried to recreate the tradition of corsetry, particularly the handmade one, and show it as outerwear. It enhances the woman's body, without mortifying her curves, but at the same time is extremely sensual, as it highlights and flatters, leaving space to the imagination, without being too revealing. Sicily, with its women and tradition, is for us an endless source of inspiration; the contrasts and passions of this land are always a starting point for us. We like to match sacred and profane elements (the guêpière and the rosary), without ever forgetting the handcraft tradition (the handmade crochet shawl), everything worn with extremely high heels.

The dress belongs to the Spring/Summer 1990 collection and since then we have featured this favorite dress in almost every collection. Corsetry is a basic and at the same time a signature Dolce & Gabbana item.

donna karan

My Favourite Dress: Donna Karan, Autumn/Winter 1996, Handmade devoré

It is always difficult to explain where the division between fashion and art lies. Our business often dictates that a designer struggles between creativity and commerciality. An evening dress is the exception. By definition, it is the ultimate single expression – created for a special purpose, a magical moment or entrance. For that reason, my hand made devore dress is my favourite dress. Starting with its artisan fabric of hand burnt patina velvet on sheer silk illusion; brushed with abstract artistic strokes – the dress's sole intention is to pay homage to the body. The alternating textures are suspended and draped on the form to seduce a woman's curves and accent her skin. The woman becomes a living, breathing sculpture immortalised not in stone, but the impression she makes. Because the fabric is handmade, each dress is one-of-a-kind. I also love this timeless dress because of its iconic association. We found the perfect woman to immortalise it in our advertising campaign, my friend Demi Moore. The fabric, the dress, the woman all came together in a sensational moment, captured for all time. To me, therein lies the art of fashion.

dries van noten

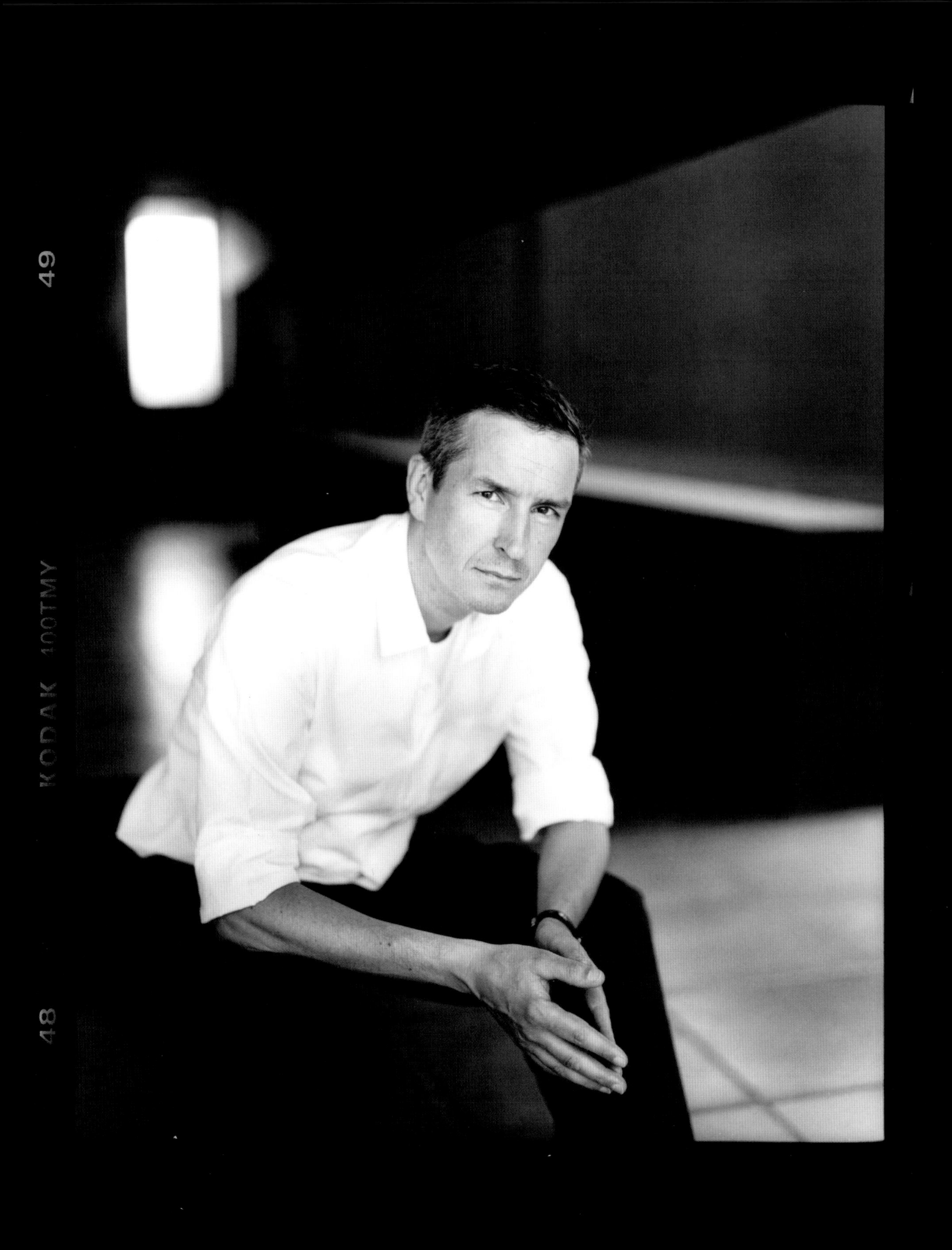
49
KODAK 100TMY
48

My Favourite Dress: Dries van Noten,
Spring/Summer 1999, Silk velvet, jewellery
with mussels

*The theme of the black dress found its
origins in the film* The Piano. *The black dress
has for me the ideal mix of tradition though
designed in a contemporary way, it has
become a favourite. I like working from a
historical, ethnical or folkloric point of view,
though bringing those sensibilities out in a
new and modern way. The mussels in the
jewellery also refer to a scene in* The Piano
*pulling the piano out of the sea, which is
covered with mussels and sea plants as
well as a reference to Belgian art.*

eley
kishimoto

Our Favourite Dress: Eley Kishimoto,
Spring/Summer 1998, Cotton pigment and
devore print

*We chose this Egg and Diamond dress as
it is the first dress we designed as Eley
Kishimoto and its strength is as strong now as
it was then. It is one of our favourite dresses.*

elie saab

My Favourite Dress: Elie Saab,
Haute Couture Collection, Autumn/Winter
2001/02, Taffeta skirt and net tulle top with
hand embroidered silk flowers and leaves

*The inspiration for the collection was
'woman meets nature'. The dresses in the
collection were created with fabrics that
gave the illusion of the wearer being
half-dressed, half-naked. Halle Berry's dress
used a mixture of fabrics. The full taffeta skirt
was made of rich silk paired with a fine
net tulle top. The breast and waist area was
covered with delicately hand embroidered
flowers and leaves so that there was a subtle
display of skin.*

*I was absolutely thrilled when Halle wore
my dress to the Oscars and when she won it,
I was even more excited. She has the perfect
colouring and figure for the dress and looked
so beautiful in it. It really was one of the
most wonderful moments of my career.*

francisco costa
for calvin klein

My Favourite Dress: Francisco Costa for Calvin Klein, Spring/Summer 2009, Silk and wool

This was the opening look of my Spring 2009 Calvin Klein Collection show and it is one of my favourite dresses to date. It is very organic with new dimensions and proportions for an elegant and beautiful, casual look. Initially, this dress looks like it could be intimidating, but it is not. The sleeves balance the modest simplicity of the shape, and simultaneously add life and soul to the dress. I think that the form and lines of this dress demystify the shape of a woman's body. In order to achieve the unique silhouettes in this collection, there was an intense focus on the textures and the precise seaming, pleating, and details. With this dress in particular, I was really energized by the lightness of the fabric and how it responded.

gianfranco ferré

My Favourite Dress: Gianfranco Ferré, Autumn/Winter 1992/93, Silk crêpe with gold foil plated cord embroideries on tulle

I have a special love of this dress because I find that it captures in perfect equilibrium the simplicity of shape and the opulence of ornamentation, the force of red (for me the ultimate colour) and the glint of gold (another all-time passion of mine). Mostly because it draws inspiration from the East, a dimension which, with its magnificent splendour, mystery and symbolism, occupies a supremely important place in my creative imagination. My East is both the East I have come to know personally, and the East which lives on in books, travel memories, fables, and fanciful tales that an unfailingly astonished and fascinated West has always produced in infinite quantity in the face of an eternal, enigmatic, exquisite civilisation.

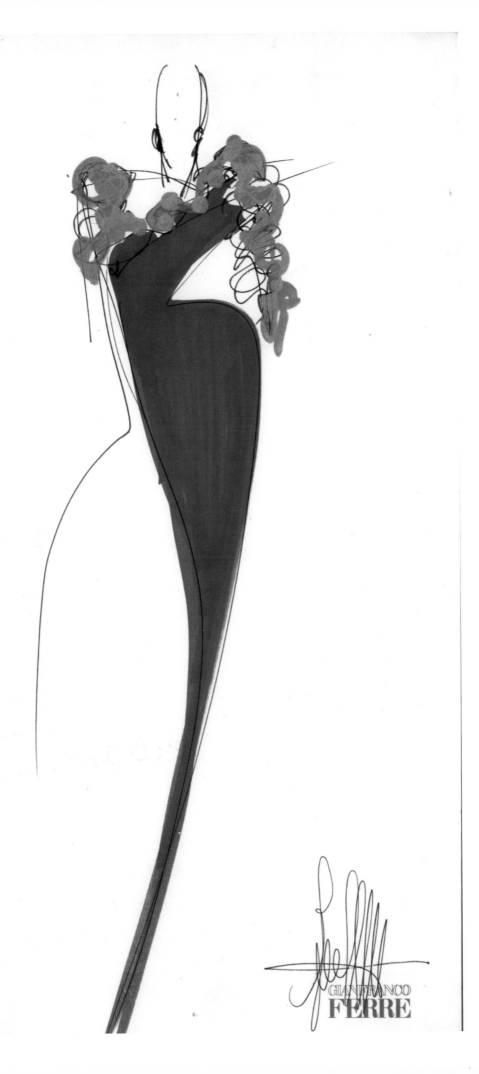

giles
deacon

My Favourite Dress: Giles,
Spring/Summer 2007, *The Car Wash Dress,*
Satin organza ghazaar with accordion
pleats and patent leather shoulder panels.

*Inspired by rotary car wash brushes. I chose
The Carwash Gown from my Spring/
Summer 2007 collection because of its
sinister structural beauty.*

"the Carwash"
2007
Spring Summer

giles
x.

giorgio
armani

My Favourite Dress: Giorgio Armani,
Spring/Summer 1999, Crystal beading
designs on silk organza

*What I particularly like about this dress
are the contrasts – it is embroidered and
yet light; it is transparent, but not obvious;
it is minimalist and yet glamorous. The colours
run into each other so that it is impossible
to define its exact colour and yet the end
result is one of harmony. It is a happy
favourite dress...*

glenda bailey

harper's bazaar
editor-in-chief

———

My Favourite Dress: Lanvin, *Resort* 2009, Crêpe de soie

Every woman should have a Madame X moment: an evening when she feels like a living, breathing work of art. For me, it was my fiftieth birthday, when I wore this Lanvin dress from Alber Elbaz's Resort 2009 collection. Alber is one of my favorite designers of all time. He knows how to make a woman feel like a goddess – and not just because he is a virtuoso at draping.
I have been known to discover a love letter embroidered in the lining of his creations; some people wear their heart on their sleeve – I wear mine on my Lanvin.

hamish
bowles
european editor-at-large
vogue

My Favourite Dress: Gabrielle "Coco" Chanel, Printemps-Été 1926, Embroidered tulle with crystal, jet and silver beads

I probably spend far too much time in the Condé Nast archives, researching stories that I am working on for Vogue, and also pieces in my costume and fashion collection. I always loved these images of Ina Claire, the piquant American actress who did much to popularize Chanel's work in America. Indeed she became something of an icon for the brand, wearing Chanel's work on stage (and later on screen) and in her private life. In fact, as Vogue's then editor Carmel Snow wrote in her autobiography, Claire eclipsed the power of society matrons to set the fashion and ushered in a new paradigm of the fashionable woman. The moment I saw this dress, at auction in New York, I knew what it was. It didn't have the Chanel label, but instead only the label for the dress salon in New York that retailed the dress – this was a period when many stores and chic specialty boutiques bought original Paris models either to duplicate in line-for-line copies or to sell directly to clients who weren't always able to travel to Paris to replenish their wardrobes. The workmanship and exquisite detailing betrays the hand of a Paris atelier. Unlabelled by Chanel, however, it had passed unnoticed through the auction room – always the most exciting moment for a collecting sleuth.

For me the holy grail of collecting is the synthesis of a dress, provenance and iconic contemporary imagery. This of course was an exciting find on many levels. To begin with I think it's a ravishing dress – the form is as modern and almost as simple as a sleeveless undershirt, but the embellishment links it to Chanel's passion for luxurious embroideries that she developed during her liaison with Russia's Grand Duke Dmitri Pavlovich. And the fact that it was photographed by Edward Steichen, the greatest fashion and portrait photographer of his day, for Vogue and on an emblematic client of the designer, makes this a special piece for me. It is also wondrous that Steichen photographed it from both the front and the (low swimsuit) back – and that Vogue published both images.

hamish
morrow

My Favourite Dress: Hamish Morrow, Autumn/Winter 2002, Web tape with wool suiting cloth

I was interested in the psychological protection that high fashion clothes afford the wearer. These types of clothes have evolved beyond mere function and are worn for reasons of desire, psychological protection and for the reinvention of the outward impression.

The industrial design of mountain climbing serves a different master. These products are no less aesthetically beautiful, but are literally created to protect the user/wearer from death whilst exposed on the rock face. Additionally clothing is suspended from the body, as the body would be suspended from the rock face, strapped into a protective harness. The juxtaposition of these two ideas, along with a desire to create new methods of suspending clothing on the body, formed the basis of the inspiration for both this particular dress and the collection in general.

The dress is draped with heavy concentration of volume on the front hip region. This would normally cause the dress to distort under the weight of the fabric. A free-form harness has been draped around the body to support the weight of cloth and thus resolves both the practicality as well as the aesthetic aspirations of the garment. In order to make the hard, industrial colour of the web tape work, it has been offset against the neutral ground of an oversized, "Prince of Wales" check, wool suiting, cloth. This particular dress encapsulates many of my own personal aspirations when investigating the body as a sight for 3-D design.

isaac mizrahi

My Favourite Dress: Isaac Mizrahi, c.1992, Wool

I think my favourite dress ever designed was a long white woollen dress with an exploded photo-real tulip printed on it, circa 1992. Those prints were so exciting to design and I feel they were widely influential.

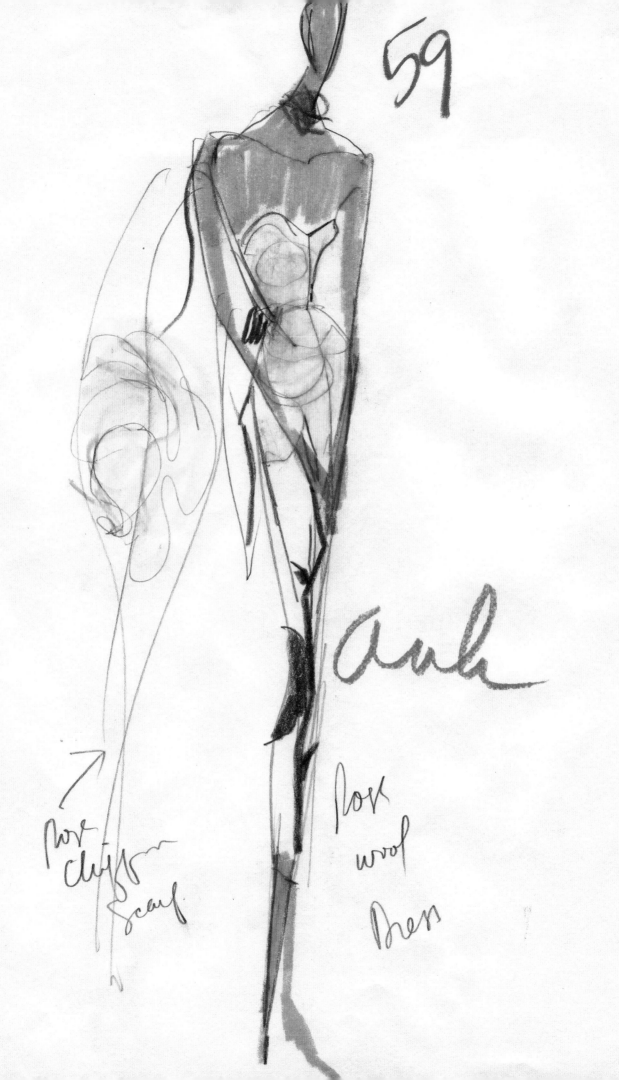

59

Azela

Rose
chiffon
scarf

Rose
wool
Dress

isabel toledo

My Favourite Dress: Isabel Toledo, 1991,
Sheer quilted organdie

*My favourite dress earns the title based on its experience
not on its beauty, design, or financial reward. This sheer
quilted organdie dress has had a long life (in fashion years).
I first made it in 1991. It seems to have as many stories as it
does embroidered squiggles. In the making, the beginning
always has an exchange of dialogue. As in the tradition of
quilt making, needle and thread expresses emotion.*

*Once the dress is delivered, different stories find their way
back. I have been told you can sleep in it, on it or use it as
a shelter. It has been a winter wedding dress - The bride
full of excitement insisted, "I was being hugged all the way
down the aisle." She is still married!*

*Because of its bigness, softness and confronting power,
this dress is a community and my "Favourite Dress".*

issey miyake

Fête dress " l'Oiseau de Paradis "
(form, when we put it flat.)

My Favourite Dress: Issey Miyake Fête, 2002
L'Oiseau de Paradis, Polyester

I have selected a dress called L'Oiseau de Paradis after one of the constellations as my favourite. The piece is one of the first of the series named after stars. The dress was cut with a newly developed and unique method that uses ultrasonic waves. This permits the hems to curve freely and puts no weight at the hem, making the dress seem weightless. The dress appears two-dimensional, but transforms unexpectedly when worn.

jane bruton
editor-in-chief
grazia magazine

My Favorite Dress: Personal archive, Silk

When I first saw this dress I thought "Hmmm, not sure – is that snooker green?" but I tried it on and have barely taken it off ever since. It's the ultimate day to night dress with a flattering scoop neck and soft figure-flattering fabric. It's feminine but strong at the same time – and it stands out because not many other people do wear green.

jasper conran

My Favourite Dress: Jasper Conran, July 1994,
Wedding dress for Lady Sarah Chatto (née Armstrong-Jones),
Silk chiffon top layer with under layers of crêpe drape, satin
organza, ghazaar and net

*I have chosen this dress because, for me, it encapsulates many
things. It was commissioned by someone whom I like very much,
Lady Sarah Chatto, who is modest and simple in her approach
to life, but who had to have a very public ceremony on her
wedding day. I had been making clothes for Sarah for years
when she asked me to make her wedding dress, but this was very
different to anything we had done before since we would have to
be in the spotlight, not something she really had to do previously.*

*The challenge, therefore, was to make a dress that would epitomise
all her qualities and give her confidence on the day itself. I also
wanted to convey a particular kind of British quality in the dress
and in the bridesmaids' dresses. A kind of quiet dignity, which had
nothing to do with the razzle dazzle of heavy frills and embroidery,
pomp, and circumstance, more England on a sunny day in the
country when the roses are in full bloom and all seems alright with
the world.*

*The whole project was such a pleasure to work on from start to
finish and the day itself was magical, both public and very private.
A designer should never be too pleased with his or her work,
but in this instance, I feel that I did my very best and cannot look at
the photographs to this day without a certain sense of satisfaction
and pleasure.*

joe
casely-hayford

My Favourite Dress: Joe Casely-Hayford, Spring/Summer 1987, Double pinstripe, cool wool with iridescent appearance, woven exclusively for the designer by Leigh Mills, Yorkshire.

The prevailing social climate plays a significant role in the direction a designer takes when developing a collection. During the mid-1980s anti fashion and deconstructionism were born out of the Punk movement, and a desire to endorse a non-aspirational style in mainstream fashion.

"My favourite dress" sums up my approach to womenswear during that very exciting time, when the content of a collection meant more than the hype that was surrounding it; before the conglomerates and the "High Street" stripped fashion of all originality and integrity. This dress was the first item of mine to gain editorial in the The Face *magazine. They called it the "Duomens" (a combination of a dress and a suit) and despite its extreme proportions my chosen dress sold very well in the UK, Italy, and Japan.*

In my view, deconstruction was a metaphor for the way in which Western society had all the right components, only they needed to be re-arranged, in order to create a more balanced solution. My Favourite Dress borrows from the idea of a woman in an oversized man's jacket; she takes on the power of its symbolism, while ridiculing the fragility of the pompous male posturing. The exaggerated shoulder line and bolero cut jacket contrast with the slim, high waisted skirt, which accentuates the female form. This creates an interesting new hybrid silhouette, a seminal 1980s garment. The fabric used was woven exclusively for me by Leigh Mills, in Yorkshire. It is lightweight, double pinstripe, cool wool, which has a lovely iridescent quality.

john galliano

My Favourite Dress: John Galliano,
Autumn/Winter 1995/96, Silk chiffon

*It was an evening in March that transformed
itself into the Winter Wonderland. The roofs
of Paris were covered in snow… The models
came out, snowflakes alighting on their
immaculate faces. It was a show where it all
came together – the beauty, the magic, the
perfect moment.*

*Then a young model emerged, her name
was Olga, it was her first season in Paris.
She was so fragile and delicate, but
embodied a strange inner strength and
beauty. Her dress was a shift of mousseline,
bias cut, with delicate roses on the shoulder.
Olga was as light as air, as pale as the
snow around her, celestial in her beauty but
in complete control of her own destiny.*

*I am an incurable romantic and I feel that
my duty is to give women a dream. I have
dedicated my whole working life to the
creation of clothing that I hope will enhance
their beauty and bring them moments of joy
to their lives. I would like to be able to help
women bring forth their personality and
individuality like in that perfect moment in
"Winter Wonderland".*

john
rocha

My Favourite Dress: John Rocha, Spring/Summer 2002,
Hand knitted leather

*The hand knitted black leather dress is without doubt one of my
very favourite pieces.*

*I have a longstanding fascination with handcraft; I take great
pleasure in working with traditional skills and giving them new
aspects and unexpected twists.*

*In this piece, I have stripped down soft leather hides and hand
knitted them into airy lines, making new shapes, patterns, and
textures. The garment is then tucked and draped to surround the
body, outlining the figure rather than hard definition of form. Set
against the volume of the taffeta underskirt, soft lines against crisp,
creating sculptural shapes.*

I love this mix, organic and yet structured, natural yet hand formed.

*I have always wanted to make beautiful things, pieces that have
longevity and enduring charm. I value the detail and care that
goes into a garment and believe these things are forever in fashion.*

julie
verhoeven

My Favorite Dress: Peter Jensen,
Spring/Summer 2009, Printed cotton jersey

I love dresses. I embrace and celebrate dresses. For the last twelve years, I have worn nothing but dresses and have banished all trousers (except studio overalls) and even skirts from my wardrobe. I must own about 100 in a multitude of prints and volumes. Coming from a place of dress worship, it is ironic I have chosen my favourite dress to be one I would not and have not worn. The dress in question was a collaboration with Peter Jensen for his Spring/Summer 2009 collection, "Jodie". It is a jersey, printed T-shirt dress, titled on its faux patch pocket, entitled As Queer as a Cat's Fart, which is a line from "Hotel New Hampshire" starring Peter's collection muse, Jodie Foster. It is joyous and upbeat in an American preppy kind of way. The bouncing billiard balls nod back to another much darker Foster film, The Accused. As does Peter's signature logo, a bunny which is up the duff, in a trailer trash kind of way. I love a T-shirt dress. They are timeless, unpretentious and have the ease and freedom of a pair of trousers. This dress is one I aspire to wear and await to be re-born with the physche of an adolescent boy, Jodie style; or the curves of Mae West to celebrate and exaggerate the female form. Long live dresses.

julien macdonald

My Favourite Dress: Julien Macdonald, Autumn/Winter 2002/03, Beading and Swarovski crystal with rabbit fur shawl

I design for confident, sexy women; women who turn heads when they walk into the room. I was inspired by sex, drugs and rock'n'roll, David Bowie, Blondie and Joan Collins.

Asymmetric, jet black beading, Swarvoski crystal and delicate lace created my favourite dress. When teamed up with a large fedora and chunky gold jewellery, the ultimate rock bitch "Look" of my collection is created.

louise goldin

My Favourite Dress: Louise Goldin, Autumn/Winter 2009, Velvet knit with Swarovski encrusted panels

This black velvet knit dress with Swarovski encrusted panels is a dress from my Autumn/Winter 2009 collection. I have worked with Swarovski for several seasons and have made some of my best pieces in collaboration with them; however, this is definitely my favourite. Even though this dress works as an amazing showpiece, it is still extremely feminine and wearable.

This dress has received numerous compliments from both men and women. It is structured in a way that refers back to my primary research on transformers, that was the original inspiration behind this collection. Yet it is worked in a way that flatters the female form, which also draws upon aspects of Zoomorphia as in inspiration for style lines, which was my secondary area of research for Autumn/Winter 2009.

My favourite feature of the dress is the way in which the stones are cut; each crystal has an eye in the centre-back that makes it extremely interesting to look at both close up and from a distance. This stone enables the Swarovski panels to appear almost fluid, creating an amazing effect and movement when the dress is worn.

luella bartley

My Favourite Dress: Luella,
Spring/Summer 2001, Cotton with car paint

*The dress was the first outfit from my Fluoro
Collection. I actually hated this dress for a
really long time after the show – pure overkill.
But then a few months ago I saw it again
for the first time in ages and loved it.
It represents for me a period when designing
the collection meant a continuous state
of overexcitement, not only did we graffiti
the dress, but my whole studio and every
telephone, notebook, table we could find.
Consequently, we all had to live very
closely with that collection for a long time
afterwards and fluoro pink car spray 'aint the
easiest thing to live with after the first month
of novelty. It was only the third collection
I had done, but the buzz was wild.
Kate Moss decided to do the show at the
last minute and suddenly we had all the
makings of our first cult item, mad colour,
the print done on a friend's computer in
about half an hour, the design inspired by a
pillowcase, with a pleat that sent the whole
thing squiffy, and lop-sided, put it on Kate
who can make a pillow case look like the
sexiest, coolest thing on Earth, and we had
managed the silliest hype. What fun.*

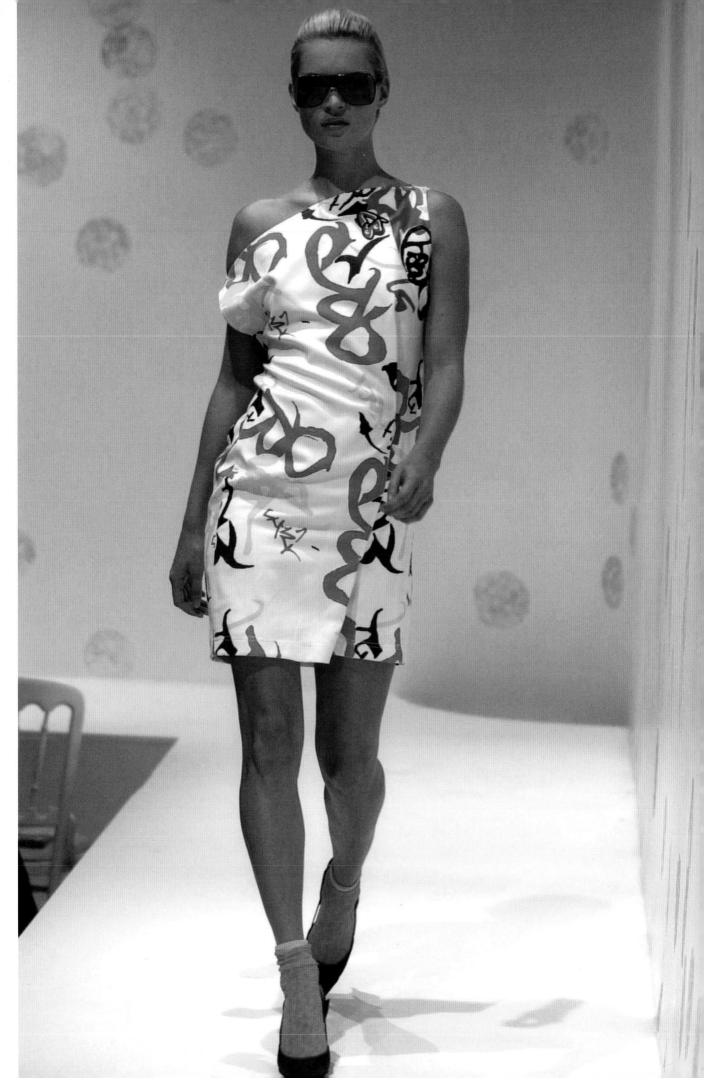

margaret howell

My Favourite Dress: Margaret Howell, Spring/Summer 1982, *Gymslip Dress*, Linen

I rarely design dresses, but when I do it is usually a functional work wear garment that I interpret to wear as a dress. My first was the "Scout's Dress", a collarless shirtdress with lots of functional pockets. Then there was the 'overall' or a wrap over dress in linen. But the most successful and photographed was the "gymslip", inspired by school uniform and navy serge. I made my own gymslip extra long in Irish shirting linen. They were worn in brown, black, white and pale pink linen and wrapped around the hip with a long stitched self-belt. It was produced in black and cream silk satin and became a dress to wear for an occasion. For the Autumn season the gymslip was made in pinstripe wool suiting to wear over a long sleeve t-shirt or a white collarless shirt and the wool version we wore with tough leather belts and flat Manolo leather boots. A classic favourite dress.

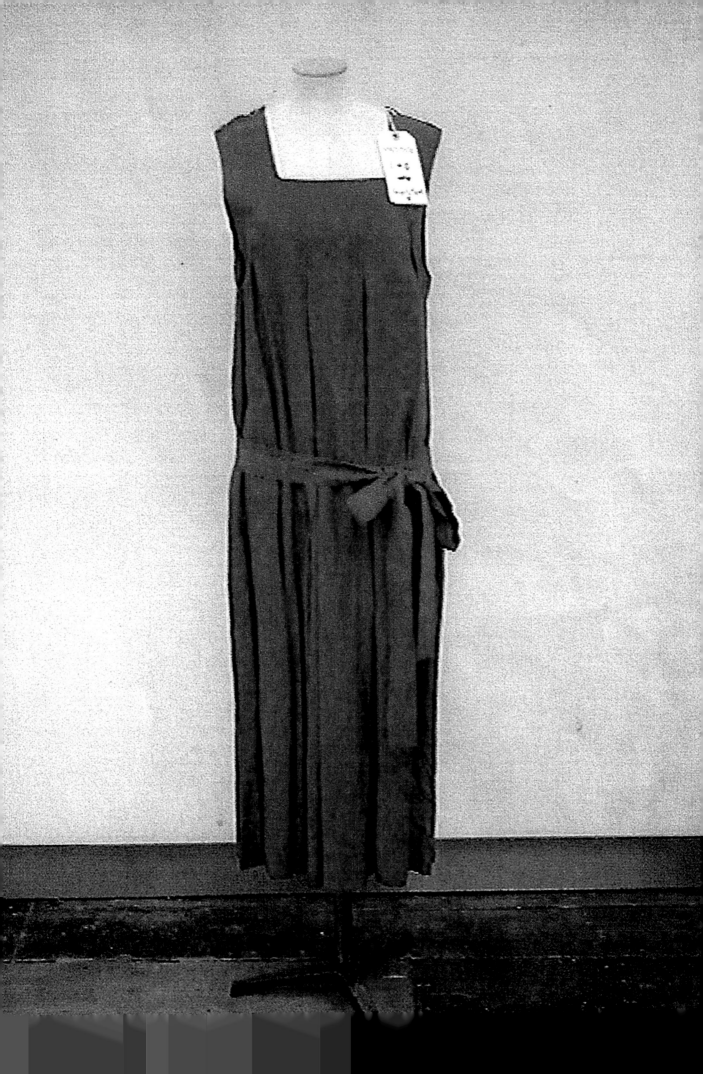

maria grachvogel

My Favourite Dress: Maria Grachvogel, Spring/Summer 2003, Silk

My favourite dress is actually this draped white silk catsuit. It was from my Spring/ Summer 2003 collection shown during Paris Fashion Week. Timeless and gorgeous, this catsuit has now been in my wardrobe for 7 years and is the piece that comes out when I am looking for effortless glamour.

I have always been a fan of catsuits, somehow they have all of the elegance of a dress, but with added versatility and an ease in wearing that cannot be understood until you try it. This one is halterneck and completely backless with a gorgeous drape and super wide flowing legs cut as a single piece of fabric which move like a dream when you walk.

markus lupfer

My Favourite Dress: Markus Lupfer,
Spring/Summer 2003, Printed silk chiffon
with cotton trimming

*This favourite dress embodies the essence of
my collection: elegant yet casual at the same
time. Contrasting elements mixed together
give the dress a special and new edge.
The feel is expressed in the light and
luxurious fabrics of wispy silk cotton with a
sexy and cool shape emphasised by sporty
details on the pockets and neckline.
The vivid colours and graphics mix into an
almost psychedelic look. Jean Shrimpton was
the main inspiration behind the collection.*

mary quant

My Favourite Dress: Mary Quant
The Daisy Dress, Knit

My favourite dress is the simplest, the Daisy Dress. This happens from working through more complex designs until the simplest solution presents itself.

The vintage "Daisy Dress" seems to have everything I want to say. It is simple, chic and sexy, and demands sensational legs, which is why I gave it to Bona Montagu. She wore it and Orlando proposed. Therefore, Bona became Bona Plunket Greene and does have the most sensational legs.

matthew williamson

My Favourite Dress: Matthew Williamson, Spring/Summer 2002, Silk georgette

It was really difficult to choose my ultimate favourite dress, because I always have a favourite from each collection. In order to make the decision I had to really think about the reasons why I like a particular piece. One of my favourite dresses is the first dress I ever made. It was a fuchsia pink and turquoise bias cut dress which Kate Moss modelled for me at my first ever show. I have fond memories of this dress as it symbolised the beginning of my career. But I wanted to pick a piece that really embodies the work that I do. I chose this nude silk georgette dress from my Spring/ Summer 2002 Collection as it really seems to capture my signature style.

I am passionate about details, and with this dress I wanted to create something which was intricately detailed and feminine, something which the wearer would want to treasure. I love the fact that this dress is totally glamorous, sparkly and eye-catching, yet it's easy shape somehow makes it more wearable and laid back. Once I had the shape right, I drew every single bead and embroidery thread myself onto the paper pattern. I sat with the beaders in India for two days and helped them create the design until it was perfect. I wanted the embroidery threads to jump out from the fleshy colour of the georgette. Everyone wondered why I chose to embroider butterflies and in truth there is no real reason other than they looked pretty. This dress has been one of my most popular pieces to date so it is nice to know those butterflies have found happy owners.

max & lubov azria
for hervé léger

Our Favourite Dress: Hervé Léger by Max Azria, Autumn/Winter 2008, *The Anthracite Dress*, Rayon, nylon and spandex knit with ribbon detail

In the Autumn of 2008 we showed Hervé Léger by Max Azria on the runway in New York for the very first time; that collection was the culmination of so much creativity, passion, and time – watching people's reactions was an intense moment of pride.

michiko koshino

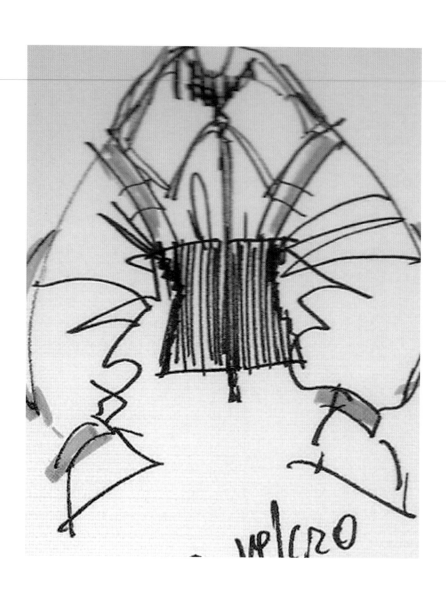

VELCRO
MUO

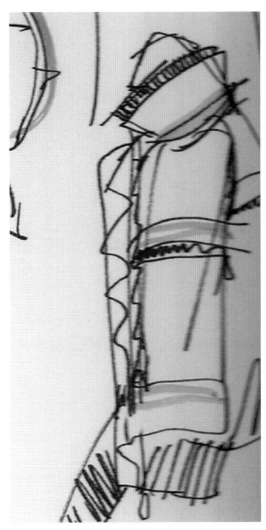

My Favourite Dress: Michiko Koshino,
Autumn/Winter 1999/2000, High performance fabric
by Schoeller, wadding

The dress was designed to celebrate the Millennium, a dress for the future. I wanted it to be a protective cover for the wearer, against any outside elements of the future. It was to be cocoon-like, enveloping and like a duvet, warm and comfortable. I worked on it for days, modifying the shape so that it looked doll-like, humorously futuristic but still feminine and curvy. I chose lightweight high tech silver fabric and added soft wadding, and as the shape grew, I joined the shoulders up towards the head and added a hood and a visor for total coverage. It is my all time favourite dress.

naoki takizawa

My Favourite Dress: Issey Miyake by Naoki Takizawa Spring/Summer 2003, Cotton jersey and high-count pleated polyester

Led by the mysterious beauty of a model I met, who was the embodiment of a woman I had seen in a Modigliani painting. I created this dress unconsciously: this was the first time for me to take such a process in my creation. This feeling left me with a pleasant subconscious sense in my memory.

The dress was introduced in the Spring/Summer Collection in Paris on the 3rd of October. It was created with a very simple structure: cotton jersey as its base together with high-count polyester. The polyester, pleated in short pitches, is made into a tape shaped fabric, and is simply arranged around and attached to the dress. As a result, a very plain structure and silhouette give this dress an elegant expression, which at the same time belies its form, which is a dress as an extension of a T-shirt created for a modern sense of value.

nicole farhi

NICOLE FARHI

My Favourite Dress: Nicole Farhi,
Autumn/Winter 2002, Habatai silk

*The nude habatai silk strip dress is my
favourite dress because it has a fabulous
quality as if it came out of a story. It has the
colour and transparency of your own skin,
and it scintillates almost as if it were alive.
It belongs in fiction, but it is also perfect to
wear in real life.*

oriole
cullen
curator
victoria & albert
museum

My Favourite Dress: Chanel evening dress, 1939,
Victoria and Albert Museum collection, Silk

In her autobiography 'In My Fashion' American Vogue editor Bettina Ballard wrote of the frenetic atmosphere of the Paris Spring Season of 1939: 'I can remember thinking, as I dressed for one entertainment or another, that there would have to be some emphatic punctuation to mark the end of this season of frenzied frivolity so that Paris could start afresh on a saner social plan.' The approaching war had become inevitable and with a last gasp the social set was determined to go down partying.

For the spring collections of that year Chanel had shown a patriotic red, white and blue 'gypsy' collection of which this dress formed a part. The combination of a modest sun-top bodice in rich red grosgrain silk and a luxuriously full, light-as-air red chiffon skirt result in a garment of simple elegance and easy wearability for which Chanel was famed. There are no superfluous ornaments, embellishments or complicated fastenings, the only decorative feature being thin straps and edgings of petersham ribbon in the colours of the tricolour: red, white and blue. A perfect dress in which to live for the moment, in which to make an entrance, to walk, run, dance, sing and party and to watch the sunrise over the Seine.

Perhaps it says something of the hope in elegance and beauty, a kind of refusal to be overcome by the direst of situations which continued throughout the war with Parisiennes using scraps of fabric ingeniously twisted into elegant turbans and old blankets fashioned into smart winter coats.

Or perhaps, it's just a great red dress and that's why its my favourite…

oscar
de la renta

My Favourite Dress: Pierre Balmain Haute Couture Crée Par Oscar de la Renta, Autumn/Winter 1997/98, Velvet embroidered coat with sable trimming, over printed silk chiffon dress

I love this look for its glamour. This sable trimmed coat over the green printed silk chiffon strapless evening dress is made of hand-embossed velvet executed in Venice in an old Fortuny technique, and then re-embroidered with gold and silver thread. Its design and style are timeless.

The combination of sumptuous materials and simple lines make it an elegant and classic piece. It is romantic and is as much of today as yesterday. It could have been worn by Catherine the Great on an amorous escapade.

osman yousefzada

My Favourite Dress: Osman Yousefzada, Spring/Summer 2009, *Hera Dress*, Neoprene bonded silk

My favourite dress, the Hera dress, is about proportions, inspired by Somalian women wrapping themselves in loose fabric on the streets of London. I took all the clutter away and was left with a very clean and modern structure. My clothes are about the evolution of clothing through migration.

paco rabanne

My Favourite Dress: Paco Rabanne,
Spring/Summer 2002, *Pearly Dress*, Plastic
sequins and mother-of-pearl shell

*The year 2001 had witnessed sinister events.
Dramas, natural disasters, terrorist attacks.
US designers were touched by the events.
The October collections for Summer
responded spontaneously and instinctively
to the tragedies with a message of peace
and harmony with white being very
important throughout the collections.
The dress symbolises the collection, but it
also resembles my work; nacre, rhizoid,
transparency, crystalline sounds.
It synthesises the romanticism of the
collection, a romanticism playing with
the feminine body, curves, graphic mood
and sensuality, but most of all a feeling
of freedom…*

paul smith

My Favourite Dress: Paul Smith,
Autumn/Winter 2002, *Union Jack Ballgown*, Velvet

*The Union Jack Ballgown was inspired by the
idiosyncratic and sometimes contradictory styling
habits of the British gentry.*

*The dress is constructed on a fitted, boned bodice,
and made completely of velvet printed scarves.
This reflects a disregard for the traditional rules not
only by its choice of components but the alternative
colour combinations used in the re-worked Union
Jack print. This elegant evening dress is a celebration
of eccentricity and a favourite.*

pearce
fionda

My Favourite Dress: Pearce Fionda,
Spring/Summer 1997, Crêpe, satin and
silk chiffon

*Our greatest and commercial success.
A celebrity favourite, culminating in a trip
to the Oscars, which is representative of
the Pearce Fionda style. The intricate spiral
and bias cut satin backed crêpe dress is
accentuated by contrast matte and shine
panelling. It unfurls into a torrent of fabric,
cascading outwards from below the knee.
Shoe string straps cross at the back and its
double-cowled neck conceals a layer of
sheerest chiffon.*

ralph
lauren

My Favourite Dress: Ralph Lauren,
Spring/Summer 2002, Beaded tulle

*I chose this dress as a favourite for its
timeless silhouette and intricate detailing.
White beading for evening feels sexy
and modern.*

rick owens

My Favourite Dress: Rick Owens,
Autumn/Winter 2004, Silk

*This favourite dress pretty much sums what
I want to say – T-shirt easiness, in a soft
warm grey, caressing a woman's lines...*

roland mouret

My Favourite Dress: RM by Roland Mouret, Autumn/Winter 2008, *The Pigalle Dress*, Wool

My favourite dress is the "Pigalle". It uses my signature folding technique – perfect for a woman with curves. It is a dress that women fall in love with, which of course makes me very happy but I don't control that, it happens by itself.

rossella jardini
for moschino

My Favourite Dress: Moschino, Autumn/Winter 2002/03, Rayon/acetate crêpe, with sequins, nylon jacket with goose down

The black crêpe dress designed for the Autumn/Winter Collection is actually a modified version of a Franco Moschino classic from 1984. For his first collection, he had made a print version, red with black polka dots, worn by model Pat Cleveland. As every Moschino fan will recall, Ms. Cleveland sauntered down the catwalk carrying a shopping bag filled with celery and tomatoes.

The nylon jacket was actually made by Alberto Aspesi, a good friend of Franco Moschino's. It is called "Moschino" because Aspesi first produced it in Hong Kong for the designer's personal use. From then on, Franco Moschino added it to his collections repeatedly, in several versions and fabrics.

These two pieces perfectly symbolize the Moschino philosophy: that nothing is a pure invention and that beautiful things are timeless, so everything can be interpreted, mixed and matched because fashion should be fun.

romeo gigli

My Favourite Dress: Romeo Gigli, Autumn/Winter 1992/93, *Limited Edition Dress*, Mesh with lasered micropaillettes

My favourite dress is from the Space Collection, which envisioned the woman of the future on the threshold of the Third Millennium. An invitation I found most intriguing, for whatever the dress I have in mind I always picture the woman in a flush of desire as rarefied and infinite as to become a metaphor for the future. Generally, when we think of the world to come, we imagine, who knows why, an utterly geometric dimension, lacking in all nuance; where the body becomes mere accessory, expressly functional. And yet disquieting too, precisely because it seems to negate gentleness, our very ability to dream. In our exultation of a higher and ultimately quite gelid intelligence, we tend to equate woman and machine. Instead, past, present or future, I prefer to not lose grasp of a woman's sensuousness.

This is why I created for her an exquisitely airy cocoon, a bow-net of rings opening wide on the figure, fashioning the space around it, enhancing it with a fine mesh fabric rich in lasered micropaillettes; a magical vision of light twinkling with every motion. I sought to make light a slave to feminine softness. Underneath, any other dress would have had no rhyme, no reason: all required was a simple black bodysuit. Not to hide the body, but to heighten the sensuality of its every step in the most abstract and elegant of forms. This is a holography dress, just as desires are pure holography.

sonia
rykiel

My Favourite Dress: Sonia Rykiel, Spring/Summer 1997, Lace and cotton knickers

I have loved hundreds of dresses from the funniest to the most serious one, from the most erotic to the most prudish. The one that touches me most and is my favourite is this lacy dress; almost nude, with topstitches as veins that run around and cling to the body like a girdle. It exhibits itself, offers itself to the world to look at with a wink. Fashion is a dress that makes a dress that makes a dress.

sophia
kokosalaki

My Favourite Dress: Sophia Kokosalaki, Autumn/Winter 2001/02, Viscose and silk with leather

I have chosen this piece from my Autumn/ Winter 2001/2002 collection, a dress using two distinctive 'signature' materials, light jersey and leather. I have selected this in particular, as it is an early exercise in draping using strong colour and also applying different techniques on leather: pleating a piece of leather on the torso and using flat perspective folding on the shoulder while the jersey softly drapes on the bodice and skirt. By juxtaposing these two materials and manipulating the leather, I opted for a garment that created a tension between their primary characteristics, the softness of jersey and strong, hard elements in leather. The result is a dress complex in construction, yet still discreet and easy to wear, with a dynamic and feminine silhouette.

sophie albou
for paul & joe

My Favourite Dress: Sophie Albou for Paul & Joe, Autumn/Winter 2009, *Attirant*, Crêpe de chine

My favourite dress is little and black, feminine, glamorous and elegant. We named it 'Attirant' which means attractive. It incorporates all the key trends for Autumn/Winter 2009; elements of the disco era with a resolute modern signature.

French style is known for its refinement, perfect cuts and designs that make women look sublime. We continue and strive to respect and preserve this philosophy. In this style we find cleanness in the cut and a fluid shape with the addition of our lively, sparkling and sensual individuality.

This style comes from the Pierre Cardin for Paul & Joe line. A partnership with the absolute french designer from the 20th Century. We both create modern contemporary styles and follow "l'air du temps" with our designs. We worked on this design with the utmost respect for Cardin's own approach, adding fresh life with my own personal touch.

The short length of the dress accentuates long legs with black leather feminine thigh-high boots. The audacity of touch is revealed by its cut away back, low back neck line with drapping for pure evening seduction. The embroidered, exaggerated sparkling shoulder accentuates her attitude and her relaxed smart elegance. Designed for Paul & Joe Women it presents a fluid shape, reflecting positive vibes and confidence in her surroundings. This style is for a seductive woman who is at ease with herself.

stella
mcCartney

My Favourite Dress: Stella McCartney,
Autumn/Winter 2003, Silk

This is my favourite dress.

stephen jones

My Favourite Dress: Stephen Jones,
St. Martins Graduate Collection, 1979, Duchess satin with
ombré chiffon and shattered perspex tiara

*How can I choose my favourite dress? As I milliner I flit
between the world's best dressmakers already. Consequently,
do I choose a Marc Jacobs abstraction, a Giles Deacon
architectural, a Galliano symphonic or a Dior iconic?
Or do I pick one of Rei's life changing designs? As fashion
designers must be autocratic, a milliner must be democratic
and therefore I can have no favourite.*

*To sidestep this issue I have taken one of my own dresses
from my St Martin's graduation fashion show thirty years
ago in 1979. Hats were merely an accessory in my
womenswear show, becoming my raison d'être only after
having left college. This formal dress was designed to be
worn at court (although presentations had been stopped
in 1958. As Princess Margaret famously said, "We had
to stop it. Every tart in London was getting in.") and was
fashioned from aerodynamic seamed duchess satin with a
billowing ombré chiffon insert. The matching dysfunctional
tiara was shattered Perspex and the traditional Prince of
Wales plumes brought up to date with a dead seagull.
Perfect for her Majesty!*

thierry mugler

1

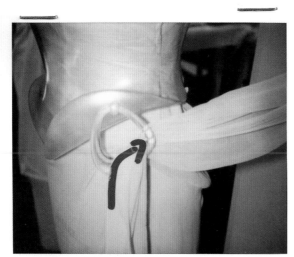

Put the floating
panel of the skirt
through the plexi
ring.

2

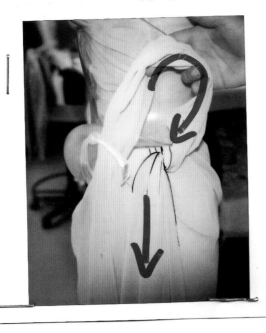

Then let the
floating panel of
the skirt through
the skirt's textile
ring (at the bottom
of the zip)

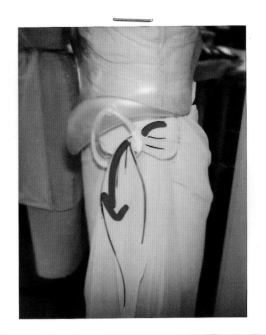

from the textile no
of the dress left the
floating panel again
through the plexi
ribs.

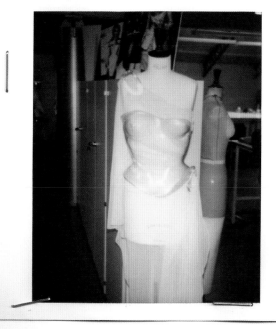

My Favourite Dress: Thierry Mugler,
Haute Couture Collection Autumn/Winter
1999/2000, *Pearly Goddess Dress*, Crystalline
sculptured bustier over shimmering pearly voile

This dress is my vision of the "Venus of the Future".
A symbol of femininity – the Birth of the Universe,
my way. It is the picture of a pure "astral body".
I like its mother of pearl aspect, which makes
the skin seem even more transparent and
creates an aura surrounding the woman. I like
the fragility of it as well which acts, nevertheless,
as a protective armour. There is a duality here
between the classicism of the dress and the
way it is being treated in a very scientific way.
I would love to see the Virgin Mary in it, with
her milky hair, ethereal skin, or Saint Blandine, a
Christian martyr thrown to the lions! I showed
this dress on a very young Russian model in
Times Square during a "Tribute to New York"
event organised by Mayor Giuliani. When she
appeared on the video screen, twenty floors
high, the whole audience – usually so rowdy –
became silent. Can you imagine? I shut Times
Square up!

tracey emin

artist &
fashion muse

My Favourite Dress: Vivienne Westwood, Taffeta

My favourite dress is my black taffeta ball gown by Vivienne Westwood. It is full skirted and has a low plunging neckline. Unlike most Westwood ball gowns it is not corseted so it is very comfortable. I wear it with a large, wide black Yves Saint Laurent belt, which gives the illusion that I have a very small waist. The thing that I like about the dress is that it looks big and really glamorous, but in reality you can wear it like a pair of jeans. In fact, on a cold winter's night you could quite easily wear a pair of jeans underneath it. It looks really cool with a short jacket on top, as well as bolero cardigans and shawls. I like to prance around in it, pretending I am in the adverts for Scottish Widows. It has a lot of a Queen Victoria/Gone With the Wind vibe. It is very romantic and sensual, as the taffeta is very soft and puffs up when someone presses against you. One of my finest occasions in the dress was rolling down a long flight of stairs at the home of Stephen Webster, the jeweller. I landed unharmed, like a big, black puffball. I wear this dress again and again, to large balls, public occasions and charity events – the only thing that is missing are a few medals! I'm sure I'll be wearing this dress for a long, long time.

tristan webber

My Favourite Dress: Tristan Webber, Autumn/Winter 2002/03, Silk poult, silk marocaine and hand-painted silk chiffon with hand appliqué chiffon patterning.

This dress was hand-constructed over three weeks using freehand embroidery techniques, after the cloth had been hand-painted and over-dyed using natural paints and dyes. The map images suggest that the dress had been constructed using damaged watermarked maps charted by history's pioneer explorers, and represent the value of knowledge. The relief surface embroidery echoes the imagery found on satellite scan of the Earth's surface, and suggests the 3-D modelling techniques of modern-day science. This dress is the combination of an historical narrative with modern science and an irreverent approach to construction.

This is my favourite dress as it represents a softer shift in my approach to construction and colour, and shows a natural move towards time invested garments.

valentino

My Favourite Dress: Valentino
Haute Couture Collection, Spring/Summer
2000, Silk tulle coat with ostrich feathers
over silk tulle dress

*A dress that I associate with one of the most
important moments of the first years of my
career: a red dress from the Autumn/Winter
Collection in 1966, worn marvellously by
Princess Pignatelli and by Veruschka in two
photographs, which I still feel are among
the most significant images of my history.
True icons of the idea of glamour that has
always permeated my work. I returned to
this design, in pink, many years later, in the
collection, A Tribute to the '60s, for Summer
2000. Elizabeth Hurley wore the dress,
impeccably, at the party when the Council of
Fashion Designers of America presented me
with their Lifetime Achievement Award.
Another very important moment of my life.*

vera wang

My Favourite Dress: Vera Wang,
2006, Bobbinet tulle

I loved the youth of Michelle Williams. I loved the colour of the dress. I loved the lipstick. Just off enough to look charming, yet sophisticated.

vivienne
westwood

My Favourite Dress: Vivienne Westwood,
Autumn/Winter 1994/95, Hand knit

*After the War, experimenting with many kinds of knitting techniques
took place: knitting by hand, by machine, with small needles, knits
to look like tweed. I feel that this dress was the epitome of this
time. As well as "The Dress" being an important part of the woman's
wardrobe, what makes this dress so special is its accessibility. You
can feel good at any occasion: at the theatre or just dinner with
a friend, add a stole in Spring or Autumn. Dress up or dress down
and you still feel and look great.*

*I love wearing it and the last time I wore it at Jerry Hall's party,
I was certainly complimented. Susie Bick and Laetitia Casta have
one. In actuality, this is not my favourite. I have a mauve version,
which is dear to me.*

zac posen

My Favourite Dress: Zac Posen, Spring/Summer 2003, *Snap Gown, Gauze silk with snap tape*

The "Snap Gown" is among my favourite dresses because it embodies my vision of clothing and women. Made of silk together with industrial-type poppers (snap tape for those in the USA), the dress exemplifies what I love to see in women: the dichotomy between their softness and their strength. It allows a woman to self-tailor and use her imagination to morph into anything she wants to become. Individuality, strong character and movement are all essential characteristics of my vision for fashion. Many of the pieces I make are convertible with snaps, buckles and reconfigurations, which facilitate individualism for the wearer. The Spring 2003 Collection in which the dress debuted was named after the Greek goddess, Circe. Circe had considerable powers including the power to transform.

The "Snap Gown" can, in fact, be reconfigured. It can be snapped into pants, a bustle can be formed: it can be left long or snapped up to a shored length. It is able to change with the mood of a woman on any given day or time. The idea of making eveningwear into utilitarian wear has always fascinated me as well, and this particular dress exemplifies that vision: the snaps themselves shimmer like body shields, almost giving the impression of gelain sequins.

zandra rhodes

My Favourite Dress: Zandra Rhodes, Spring/Summer 1974,
Printed silk chiffon with *Ayers Rock* print and quilted rayon satin band

I designed this dress at the end of 1973. It was first shown in the Rocky Horror Theatre in the King's Road in the Australian Collection 1973. The print "Ayers Rock" is based on drawings I did in the Australian Outback: Ayers Rock at sunset and sunrise and the pincushion spinifex grass everywhere around it, the resulting print is in twentieth century toile de jouy style.

Then came the chiffon drape around the body slashing into the fabric with the cuts running in all the different directions of the print. Then finally designing the quilted satin top panel, which holds the whole dress together. This took several dresses to perfect, so that it moulds itself to the body and does not gape.

It turned out to be a timeless style, re-inventing itself in different disguises and in different prints, later becoming the one-sided dress in the cowboy collection with the new print "Cactus Everywhere" and once lowering itself to reveal one breast.

In this dress is true glamour, it makes a woman a statue. It has become a classic. Barry Lategan immortalised it when he did a whole group of these as Grecian statues for Vogue. Both Jackie Kennedy Onassis and her sister Princess Lee Radziwell possessed one.

It is my favourite dress because I never tire of it and I can go back to it again, and again. This dress looks wonderful on whoever wears it, big or small. It is a master of disguise and glamourises any wearer and looks good in any colourway, be it flame red satin with geranium red chiffon printed with lavender, orange and yellow or black chiffon with salmon and powder blue with salmon satin bodice or even pure pernod green.

MY *FAVOURITE DRESS*
afterword

Zandra Rhodes CBE
Fashion and textile designer

Everyone has a favourite dress, for this very reason *My Favourite Dress* was chosen to be the opening exhibition at the Fashion and Textile Museum, London in May 2003. The notion of "my favourite dress" is an all encompassing subject, which is of interest to almost everyone, not just fashion groupies; many can be interested and have an opinion – No one can be impartial – Can they?

Turning my colourful dream of founding the Fashion and Textile Museum in London into reality was no easy feat. We needed a strong exhibition, an homage to all fashion designers and fashionistas out there, on a subject that various designers would be interested in and an item that they all had in common – a dress. The designers in the exhibition had to forget their prejudices and choose a dress to represent them and their personal style amongst the glitterati of international fashion designers; this was to be a show to announce there was a new international fashion museum.

The *My Favourite Dress* exhibition did just this – it brought together a large group of designers like this fabulous book does, where the designers shine as individuals and their thoughts are immortalized just as they were in the opening exhibition. However, this book expands on this simple question and theme, bringing together a larger contingent that includes personalities from the entire fashion industry bringing their personal choice to light and preserving their dresses and thoughts forever.

authors

Gity Monsef has had over a decade of experience as a creative director, curator and author in the fashion industry. She was a key figure in the strategic development of London's first museum dedicated to contemporary fashion and textiles with founder fashion icon Zandra Rhodes. During her time at the museum the exhibition programme was listed in *Art Review*, *Time Out* and *Modern Art* in the top five shows to see segment and the education department won the Monte Blanc Award for Education. Currently, she works as an executive producer in Glass Loves, a company she founded in 2007 specialising in the development of digital content focused on fashion and film. Her last publication was the retrospective catalogue entitled *Zandra Rhodes: A Lifelong Love Affair with Textiles* (Antique Collectors' Club, 2005).

Samantha Erin Safer was Assistant Curator of the Fashion and Textile Museum working on several exhibitions such as *My Favourite Dress, Zandra Rhodes: A Life Long Love Affair with Textiles, Identity: Celebrating 25 Years of i-D Magazine*, as well as various travelling exhibitions around Europe. She was also research assistant on *New York Fashion Now* at the Victoria and Albert Museum and a contributing author to *Lucile Ltd: London, Paris, New York and Chicago: 1890-1930s* (V&A Publishing, 2009) and *Grace Kelly Style* (V&A Publishing, 2010). Samantha holds two masters degrees, one from the Royal College of Art and the other from the London College of Fashion. Currently she works for the V&A as well as lecturing in fashion history and theory.

At 35, **Robert de Niet** has worked for over 20 years as an art director, designer and typographer, with clients including BBC TV, Citibank, Diesel, the Fashion & Textile Museum, M&C Saatchi, Nobody Jeans, Stüssy, the V&A, Virgin Mobile and Walt Disney. He was Art Director for the book *Zandra Rhodes: A Lifelong Love Affair with Textiles*, magazines *SuperBlow*, *Segue*, *What* and *This Room Is Full Of Kunst*. He is currently Senior Lecturer in Visual Communication for Fashion Journalism at the University for the Creative Arts at Epsom and London College of Fashion, specializing in magazine culture and history.

photo credits

Cover: Corinne Day/Maconochie Photography

Alix Malka/Trunk Archive

Pg.1 Courtesy of Suzy Menkes

Pg.4 Ossie Clark and Celia Birtwell, Getty Images

Pg.9 Fun Ride/Sun Dress A.E. French/Archive Photos/ Getty Images

Pg.13 Craig McDean/ Art + Commerce

Alber Elbaz for Lanvin*
Portrait: David Sims, Courtesy of Lanvin
Dress: Frederique Dumoulin

Alberta Ferretti*
Portrait: Stefano Guindani
Dress: Stefano Guindani

Alexander McQueen*
Portrait: Ann Deniau
Dress: Alexander McQueen Archive

Amanda Wakeley*
Portrait: Courtesy of Amanda Wakeley
Dress: Marcia Madeira

Angela Missoni*
Portrait: Courtesy of Missoni
Dress: Chris Moore†

Anna Sui*
Portrait: Tim Schaffer
Dress: Tim Schaffer

Anne Valerie Hash
Portrait: Robert Lacow
Dress: Naarten Castelain

Antonio Berardi*
Portrait: Mark Hom
Dress: Stefano Guindani

Antony Price*
Portrait: Courtesy of Antony Price
Dress: Courtesy of Antony Price

Barbara Hulanicki
Portrait: Courtesy of Barbara Hulanicki
Dress: Courtesy of Barbara Hulanicki

Bella Freud
Portrait: Mary McCartney
Dress: John Akehurst

We would like to take this chance to thank Chris Moore at catwalking.com for all his help with these images.

* Denotes designer had been in FTM exhibition
† www.catwalking.com

Ben de Lisi*
Portrait: Courtesty of Ben de Lisi
Dress: Tim Griffiths

Bernhard Willhelm
Portrait: Marleen Daniels
A Dress for Two, Carmen Freudenthal/Elle Verhagen
A Dress for a Box, Maria Ziegelboeck
A Dress for Bernhard, Maria Ziegelboeck
A Dress for Bjork, Nick Knight
A Dress for Dead, Ronald Stoops
A Dress for Jutta, Maria Ziegelboeck

Betsey Johnson*
Portrait: Ngoc Minh Ngo
Dress: Courtesy of Betsey Johnson

Betty Jackson*
Portrait: Andrew Lamb
Dress: John Swanell

Boudicca
Portrait: Tomoka Suwa
Dress: Justin Smith

Calvin Klein*
Portrait: Peter Lindbergh
Dress: Dan Lecca
Carolina Herrera*
Portrait: Arthur Elgort
Dress: George De Soto/Getty Images Entertainment

Caroline Charles*
Portrait: Robyn Beeche
Dress: Niall McInerney, Courtesy of Caroline Charles

Catherine Malandrino*
Portrait: Wendelien Daan
Dress: Tim Griffiths

Christian Lacroix*
Portrait: Guido Mocafico
Dress: Guy Marineau

Clements Ribeiro*
Portrait: Tim Griffiths
Dress: Tim Griffiths

Daisy de Villeneuve
Portrait: Daisy de Villeneuve
Dress: Barry Lategan

David Sassoon*
Portrait: Courtesy of David Sassoon
Dress: Roxanne Lowitt

Diane Pernet
Portrait: Michael James O'Brien
Dress: Diane Pernet
Dress: Chris Moore†

Diane von Furstenberg*
Portrait: Tim Boxer/Hulton Archive/Getty Images
Dress: Roger Prigent

Dolce and Gabbana*
Portrait: Mario Testino, Courtesy of Dolce & Gabbana
Dress: Courtesy of Dolce & Gabbana

Donna Karan*
Portrait: Courtesy of Donna Karan
Dress: Peter Lindbergh/Filomeno

Dries van Noten*
Portrait: Courtesy of Dries Van Noten
Dress: Courtesy of Dries Van Noten, photographer Patrice Stable

Eley Kishimoto*
Portrait: Wakako Kishimoto Courtesy of Eley Kishimoto
Dress: Courtesy of Eley Kishimoto

Elie Saab*
Portrait: Courtesy of Elie Saab
Dress: Jeff Kravitz/Film Magic/Getty Images

Francisco Costa for Calvin Klein
Portrait: Courtesy of Calvin Klein, Inc.
Dress: Dan Lecca

Gianfranco Ferré*
Portrait: Aldo Castoldi
Dress: Aldo Castoldi

Giles Deacon
Portrait: Lee Jenkins
Dress: Chris Moore†

Giorgio Armani*
Portrait: Armani Archive
Dress: Chris Moore†
Dress: Albert Watson, Courtesy of Giorgio Armani

Glenda Bailey
Portrait: Patrick Demarchelier, Courtesy of Glenda Bailey
Dress: Stephane Gallois

Hamish Bowles
Portrait: Courtesy of Condé Nast
Dress: Metropolitan Museum of Art
Dress: Corbis / Condé Nast

Hamish Morrow*
Portrait: Stefan Ziesler
Dress: Chris Moore†

Isaac Mizrahi
Portrait: Courtesy of Isaac Mizahi
Dress: Courtesy of Isaac Mizahi

Isabel Toledo*
Portrait: Toledo Studio/Ruvan Afanador,
Dress: Courtesy of Toledo Studio

Issey Miyake*
Portrait: Yuriko Takagi
Dress: Yasuaki Yoshinaga

Jane Bruton
Portrait: Gustavo Papaleo
Dress: Courtesy of Jane Bruton and Grazia

Jasper Conran*
Portrait: Tessa Treager
Dress: Tim Graham/Getty Images

Joe Casely-Hayford*
Portrait: Ben Weller
Dress: Martin Brading

John Galliano*
Portrait: Paolo Roversi, Courtesy of John Galliano
Dress: Patrice Stable, Courtesy of John Galliano

John Rocha*
Portrait: Simon Brown
Dress: Chris Moore†

Julie Verhoeven
Portrait: Robert Bellamy
Dress: Chris Moore†

Julien Macdonald*
Portrait: Courtesy of Julien Macdonald
Dress: Chris Moore†

Louise Goldin
Portrait: Chris Moore†
Dress: Chris Moore†

Luella Bartley*
Portrait: David Sims, Courtesy of Luella Bartley
Dress: Chris Moore†

Margaret Howell*
Portrait: Miriam Renshaw
Dress: Margaret Howell Studio

Maria Grachvogel*
Portrait: Dan Stevens
Dress: Courtesy of Maria Grachvogel

Markus Lupfer*
Portrait: James Mooney
Dress: Chris Moore†

Mary Quant*
Portrait: David Bailey
Dress: Courtesy of the Fashion and Textile Museum

Matthew Williamson*
Portrait: Neil Gavin,
Dress Chris Moore†

Max & Lubov Azria for Hervé Léger
Portrait: David Callichio
Dress: TKE Productions

Michiko Koshino*
Portrait: Courtesy of Michiko Kishino
Dress: Chris Moore†
Dress: Courtesy of Michiko Kishino

Naoki Takizawa*
Portrait: Yuichi Matsuki
Dress: Chris Moore†/Naoki Takizawa for Issey Miyake Europe
SA

Nicole Farhi*
Portrait: Mitchell Sams
Dress: Mitchell Sams

Oriole Cullen
Portrait: Courtesy of the V&A
Dress: V&A images

Oscar de la Renta*
Portrait: Courtesy of Oscar de la Renta
Dress: Courtesy of Videopolis

Osman Yousefzada
Portrait: Mitchell Sams
Dress: Mitchell Sams

Paco Rabanne*
Portrait: Nathaniel Goldberg/Art+Commerce
Dress: Chris Moore†

Paul Smith*
Portrait: Sandro Sodano
Dress: Chris Moore†

Pearce Fionda*
Portrait: Dan Stevens
Dress: Chris Moore†

"My Favourite Dress...

the prevailing social climate plays a significant role in the direction a designer takes when developing a collection. During the mid-1980's anti fashion & deconstruction were born out of the punk movement & the need to endorse a non-aspirational style in mainstream fashion.

My favourite dress sums up my approach to womenswear during that very exciting period, when the content of a collection meant more than the hype that surrounded it. Before the conglomerates & the "High Street" stripped fashion of all originality & integrity. This dress was the first item of mine to gain editorial in the "Face" magazine. They called it the "Doormens". Half suit half ...

... and in the face of that ... a sign of style ... It's extreme ... een dress sold ... ue Italy & Japan. ... struction was a ... way in which western ... he right components, ... d to be re-arranged ... ate a more balanced ... favourite dress borrows ... of a woman in an oversized ... She takes on the power ... ssism while ridiculing ... lity of the pompous middle class ... e exaggerated shoulder line ... o suit jacket contrast with ... waisted skirt, which

R.M.

This creates an un... ... ybrid silhouette. ... rment. The fa... ... en exclusively for ... Yorkshire. It is ... ble pinstripe, ... an iridescent

JOE

In order to make the bland, industrial colour of the web tape work it has been offset against the neutral ground of an oversized 'Prince of Wales' check, wool suiting, cloth. This particular dress encapsulates many of my own personal aspirations when investigating the body as a subject for

'My Favourite Dress'
20 January 2003

Hamish Morrow

I was interested in the psychological protection that high fashion clothes afford the wearer. These types of clothes have evolved beyond mere function and are worn for reasons of desire, psychological protection and for the re-invention of the outward impression.

The industrial design of mountain climbing serves a different master. These products are no less aesthetically beautiful but are literally created to protect the way/wearer from death whilst exposed on the rock face.

Additionally clothing is suspended from the body, as the body would be suspended from the rock face, strapped into a protective harness. The juxtaposition of these two ideas along with a desire to create new methods of suspending clothing on the body formed the basis of the inspiration for both this particular dress and the collection in general.

The dress is draped with heavy concentration of volume on the front hip region. This would normally cause the dress to distort under the weight of the fabric. A free-form harness has been draped around the body to support the weight of the cloth and this resolves both the practicality as well as the aesthetic aspirations of the garment.

GORGEOUS TWIN!
... ON YOUR MUSEUM!
... ER TO SEE IT. I'M
... AT YOU WAN
... ROM ME.
... HT THIS BONKE,
... D OUTFIT. WOULD
... IT'S MINE FROM
... ALLEY CAT" BY B
... AROUND 1972-
... HOPE YOU'RE WELL
... YOU'RE LOOKING
... REAT! I LOVE TO RU
... SOMEDAY!
... OVE, BETSEY

DIANE VON FURSTEN...

the wrap dress in the link ... print worked many years ago ... a whole generation ... the wrap dress, a favorite ... the body - sculpts it ... allow ... the fabric, silk jersey is soft ... shiny and dry enough to ho... geometrics & solids but it's ... It is a mesmerizing dress ... longer, but on the body ... the personality of the ... It gives women confide... step to beauty ... feel exuberant! ... ... So ... feel sexy